Strategies for Struggling Readers and Writers

Step by Step

2nd Edition

Maria J. Meyerson
University of Nevada, Las Vegas

Dorothy L. Kulesza
Clark County School District, Las Vegas, Nevada

PEARSON

Merrill
Prentice Hall

Upper Saddle River, New Jersey
Columbus, Ohio

Library of Congress Cataloging-in-Publication Data

Meyerson, Maria J.
  Strategies for struggling readers and writers: step by step / Maria J. Meyerson,
Dorothy L. Kulesza.
     p. cm.
  Includes bibliographical references.
  ISBN 0-13-118177-7
   1. Reading. 2. Reading—Remedial teaching. I. Kulesza, Dorothy L. II. Title.
  LB1573.M454 2006
  372.41—dc22   2004063178

Vice President and Executive Publisher: Jeffery W. Johnston
Senior Editor: Linda Ashe Montgomery
Senior Editorial Assistant: Laura Weaver
Development Editor: Kathryn Terzano
Senior Production Editor: Mary M. Irvin
Design Coordinator: Diane C. Lorenzo
Production Coordination and Text Design: Becky Barnhart, Carlisle Publishers Services
Cover Designer: Jason Moore
Cover Image: Images.com
Production Manager: Pamela D. Bennett
Director of Marketing: Ann Castel Davis
Marketing Manager: Darcy Betts Prybella
Marketing Coordinator: Brian Mounts

This book was set in Palatino by Carlisle Communications, Inc., and was printed and bound by Banta Book Group. The cover
was printed by Coral Graphic Services, Inc.

Person Prentice Hall™ is a trademark of Pearson Education, Inc.
Pearson® is a registered trademark of Pearson plc
Prentice Hall® is a registered trademark of Pearson Education, Inc.
Merrill® is a registered trademark of Pearson Education, Inc.

Pearson Education Ltd., *London*   Pearson Education Australia Pty. Limited, *Sydney*
Pearson Education Singapore Pte. Ltd.   Pearson Education North Asia Ltd., *Hong Kong*
Pearson Education Canada, Ltd., *Toronto*   Pearson Educacion de Mexico, S.A. de C.V.
Pearson Education–Japan, *Tokyo*   Pearson Education Malaysia Pte. Ltd.
Pearson Education, *Upper Saddle River, New Jersey*

10 9 8 7 6 5 4 3 2 1
ISBN   0-13-118177-7

PREFACE

For many students in U.S. classrooms, learning to read does not happen automatically or easily. The reasons that students may struggle with reading are numerous. Regardless of the reasons, however, classroom teachers are faced with the responsibility of assisting each and every student to become literate.

Even the most successful readers may struggle with reading at times. Take, for example, the average adult trying to comprehend tax laws. Every year, millions of Americans file their income taxes. The complexity of the instructions and tax laws on which they are based put many literate adults at a disadvantage. Many of us solve this reading problem by hiring "experts" who specialize in this form of reading comprehension. We, as teachers, not only serve as "experts" for helping readers who struggle but also provide them with tools to help them learn to solve their own reading puzzles.

OUR PROFESSIONAL PERSPECTIVE

One way to consider the needs of struggling readers is in relationship to what the most successful readers do. Given any text that readers may encounter—from a grocery list to the most complex physics treatise—successful readers are motivated to complete the task, read with a fluency that results from automatic decoding, and comprehend the given text. When any one of these components is not at an optimal level, or a combination of them are out of sync, readers will struggle and likely be unsuccessful at their reading task.

We offer these research-based strategies to help struggling readers and writers become successful readers and writers. Tutors at the Literacy Development Center at the University of Nevada, Las Vegas, preservice teachers in our literacy methods classes, and practicing teachers in their own classrooms have used these strategies successfully with students. We are aware, however, that not all strategies work with all students. It is, therefore, necessary for you, the novice or veteran teacher, to continue to increase your repertoire of effective strategies and to select those that fit your students' needs. We hope our book assists you in this endeavor.

CHANGES TO THE SECOND EDITION

We have expanded this new edition in several ways. First, we begin our book with ideas on assessment, specifically its relationship to instruction, and provide tools for observing and interviewing students.

Second, we have included writing strategies throughout the book. Reading and writing both are meaning-making endeavors; students who struggle with literacy may benefit greatly from an approach that helps them understand the relationship between reading and writing and how one reinforces the other.

Third, we have incorporated strategies for English language learners. Most school districts in the United States are affected by the influx of English language learners: students from the Dominican Republic arrive in Miami; students from Russia arrive in Chicago; students from the Philippines arrive in Las Vegas; and students from Mexico arrive in Los Angeles. Monolingual classroom teachers are challenged to find effective ways to teach students to read and write in English as well as help them succeed in the content areas. We hope that our suggestions will aid you in your goal to teach all students to be literate.

Finally, we have included additional strategies that are helpful to teachers of middle school students. The amount and type of reading and writing required in middle school often overwhelms these students. We firmly believe that all teachers are teachers of literacy; science, mathematics, social studies, and literature teachers can easily incorporate our suggestions into their repertoires.

Regardless of the way in which the political wind may blow, those of us who work with students who struggle to read and write continue to seek better ways to help these students succeed. As Allington's research confirms (2002), "Good teachers, effective teachers, matter much more than particular curricular materials, pedagogical approaches, or 'proven programs'" (p. 740). We agree, not only because there is research to support this, but because of the hundreds of students at the Literacy Development Center at UNLV who have become successful readers as the result of working with good teachers.

TEXT ORGANIZATION

To facilitate the use of the strategies, we have organized them into four areas of literacy: *motivation, word recognition, comprehension*, and *fluency*. These four areas of literacy, as well as the strategies described, work in unity. Improvement in one area will most likely lead to improvement in another area. Assessment tools specific for each of the four areas are also included in each section. A general format for all strategies follows:

- general information about the strategy
- reasons for its effectiveness with struggling readers, referred to as the "power" of the strategy
- steps to follow

- using the strategy with English language learners
- using the strategy to improve writing
- application and examples
- teaching aids and professional references.

We hope, in addition to using the ideas presented in our book, classroom teachers and reading specialists will keep in mind that students will be successful readers and writers when these strategies are used in conjunction with a comprehensive literacy program that includes:

- students engaging in activities that include reading and writing at least 50% of the school day
- students reading texts that are at their instructional level as well as text that they can easily comprehend
- students working in classrooms where teachers model the thinking of good readers and writers
- students discussing concepts, hypotheses, and strategies with their teachers
- students choosing assignments that are designed to challenge them
- students receiving grades based on their effort and improvement (Allington, 2002)

Acknowledgments

We wish to thank our families, friends, and professional colleagues who continued to encourage us as we revised our book. Most important, we wish to thank our students; they continue to help us refine our practices. We also wish to thank Linda Montgomery, our editor, and the following reviewers of our manuscript for their comments and insights: Debbie East, Indiana University; Carolyn Hannum, Concordia University, Ann Arbor; Sandra Rollins Hurley, The University of Texas at El Paso; Kathleen Jonson, University of San Francisco; Janet Kehe, Upper Iowa University; and Michele Southerd, Illinois State University.

Maria J. Meyerson
Dorothy "Dottie" Kulesza

Reference

Allington, R. (2002). What I've learned about effective classroom teaching from a decade of studying exemplary elementary school teachers. *Phi Delta Kappan, 83*(10), 740–747.

CONTENTS

PART IV

When Struggling Readers and Writers Need to Improve Fluency   63

PART V

When Struggling Readers and Writers Need to Improve Comprehension   85

APPENDIX

Additional Forms May Be Reproduced for Classroom Use   119

About the Authors

Maria J. Meyerson, Ph.D., is a professor of literacy education at the University of Nevada, Las Vegas (UNLV). With more than 25 years in education, Meyerson is a former remedial reading teacher for the Buffalo Public Schools and the Clark County School District. She served as the director of the Literacy Development Center at UNLV for 10 years, working with children, preservice teachers, and master and doctoral students. She continues to work with the Paradise Professional Development School as well as other schools in the Las Vegas area.

Dorothy L. Kulesza, Ed.D., is called "Dottie" by all who know her. She completed her doctorate in 2001. Dottie was a classroom teacher and literacy specialist at the Paradise Professional Development School. After two years as a visiting professor at UNLV, she was a Humanities teacher with the Clark County School District as well as a part-time literacy instructor. Dottie recently accepted a position as Assistant Principal at Goolsby Elementary School and Christensen Elementary School in Las Vegas, Nevada.

PART I

The Importance of Assessment

Assessment is the cornerstone of good instruction; classroom teachers and reading specialists must determine the strengths and needs of their students through informal and formal assessment procedures, and evaluate that information before instruction begins. In this text, we have incorporated specific assessment information into each of the chapters on motivation, word recognition, comprehension, and fluency so that stronger ties are made between assessment and instruction.

In our opinion, the most effective assessment tools are those that provide teachers with information about students in a timely manner. The more current the data, the more likely instructional decisions will match individual students' needs. Standardized tests are used to measure how students compare with each other (norm-referenced) or how much of a particular curriculum they have learned (criterion-referenced). The information is valuable to teachers and schools for long-range planning. Too often, however, standardized test results are not reported to teachers for several months. In addition, standardized tests usually include only a few questions on any particular topic (FairTest). For these reasons, standardized tests do not provide the best information for teachers to make instructional decisions for individual students. Our focus, then, will be on those assessment tools usually referred to as alternative, informal, or authentic assessments.

OBSERVING STUDENTS IN ACTION

As a classroom teacher or reading specialist, you know a great deal about the students you teach just by observing them in action. For example, if a student repeatedly takes an inordinate amount of time to "find" a book for silent reading, the teacher may consider that "lack of motivation or

1

interest" are factors interfering with task success. Or, a student who eagerly begins reading but appears frustrated after a page or two may be motivated, but is not sure how to select an appropriate book for independent reading.

Observation is not an easy task, however. Without a focus or purpose, observation is haphazard and the data collected may be misleading or useless. Mary Jane Drummond, in her wonderful book *Learning to See: Assessment Through Observation* (1994), details the complexities of observations. "The complexity of classroom events may sometimes mean that careful scrutiny of one part of the scene may blot out an awareness of the other equally important elements in the picture" (p. 17). Drummond also suggests that teachers who observe students must switch their focus from their own teaching to the students' learning. During a conversation with a group of elementary teachers about what they included in their literacy programs, one teacher stated that she already scheduled 2 hours per day to literacy instruction. Drummond most likely would suggest that teachers examine the amount of time *each student* is engaged in literacy and not focus on the amount of time scheduled in the teacher's plan book.

Observation takes time and requires you to examine your daily schedules to find the opportunities to observe. By observing the students who are struggling in reading and writing, you can gain insights into students' behaviors and instructional needs that may not be apparent through other means. For example, the reasons a student seldom completes the required center activities may include "off task" behavior. Observing that student in action may reveal that the student can't read the directions and, thus, keeps bothering other students.

The Literacy Observation

The Literacy Observation (Meyerson, 1997) procedure will help you make interpretations of students' affective, cognitive, and conative (determination, persistence, and will) behavioral development. To use the Literacy Observation, follow these steps:

1. Select a student to observe at least three times for approximately 10 minutes each time he/she is engaged in a literacy activity. Try to spread your observations over several days. Try to avoid letting the student know you are observing him/her.

2. Write anecdotal notes while observing. Try to record as much as possible of what you see as if you are a camera. What exactly is the student doing? Where is the student in relation to other students? and so forth. Do not "interpret" while observing.

3. Summarize the notes using the observation form (Figure 1.1). After summarizing, consider what the student's behavior could imply in terms of affective, cognitive, and/or conative literacy development.

Student's Name _____ Grade _____

Observer _____ Setting _____

Date   Summary of Observed Behavior   Implications

_____

FIGURE 1.1   Observation Form.

Student's Name _Raymond_____ Grade ___1_____

Observer _Melanie_____ Setting _ Mrs. Field's Classroom_____

Date   Summary of Observed Behavior   Implications

_____

| 5/28/98 | "Reading Rotations": Raymond is being observed doing individual reading in a group of six on the floor. He is sitting, looking around, with his book on his lap, opened to the correct story. The teacher calls on Raymond next to read aloud to her. Raymond loses his place in the book, then quickly fumbles through the stories. Teacher assists him. Raymond reads the title of the story and the first few words in a very low voice. He stops, then struggles with every other word. The teacher tells him the words he doesn't get. | Raymond seems to be struggling with fluency in reading this particular story. It appears that he has low self-confidence in literacy. The story he was reading was a repetitive story; however, Raymond doesn't seem to pick up on the patterns. This tells me that he might possibly need more experience with the story, or it is just beyond his instructional reading level because he struggles with too many words. Maybe the teacher should have made the story more familiar to Raymond by reading the story aloud together a number of times (maybe she has?), or have him read an easier story. Raymond does appear to have some literacy strengths. For example, he knows individual words have meaning, he knows where to begin the story, and he knows to read the text from left to right. He does seem to lack strategy skills for figuring out words to self-correct instead of depending on the teacher to do it for him. |

FIGURE 1.2   Example of Completed Observation Form.

4. Write an overall statement of the student's literacy activities, noting any patterns that you may see over the different observations. What do these behaviors imply for literacy instruction?

In Figure 1.2 Melanie, a classroom teacher, observed Raymond during "reading rotations" (reading centers). Note how Melanie is aware that her observation is limited to what she sees at the time but that she is nonetheless able to document some of Raymond's literacy strengths.

The Literacy Interview

The Literacy Interview (Meyerson, 1997) is another useful tool through which you can gain insights into students' understanding of the broad social purposes of literacy (Appendix Form 1B). We use this interview regularly at UNLV's Literacy Development Center.

The Literacy Interview is administered one-on-one. After establishing rapport, ask the student to answer the five questions as completely as possible while recording the responses verbatim. Tape recording the interview can be useful, especially with older students who may give lengthy responses.

From a theoretical perspective, literacy is the foundation for all education. For this reason, we found Walmsley's (1991) four educational ideology categories appropriate to guide the analysis of the Literacy Interview results. In addition to Walmsley's categories, we found a fifth category that emerged from the responses of students at the Center (Figure 1.3). Use these categories to analyze questions 1 through 4.

- *Cultural transmission (CT)* defines the purpose of education as the passing on of knowledge from one generation to another via either an academic perspective (reading literature and sophisticated written

---

Response Guidelines

Questions 1–4

CT Cultural transmission
"To learn my alphabet"
"To write bills"
"People need it for life like lawyers and doctors"
"Sound out letters and say them and put them together"

CD Cognitive development
"People read to learn stuff"
"To learn how to be smart"

E Emancipatory—social/political change
"So you can vote"
"To be able to know what the government says"
"So people don't think I am an alien"

SI Social interaction
"Because people miss each other they write letters"
"To make people happy"

R Romantic/student-centered
"Writing is showing your ideas and feelings"
"When you write you put your thoughts and feelings down"

N No response

Question 5

Anthropological	(e.g., using rocks and stones, writing on walls)
Inventions	(e.g., people invented books and pencils)
Cognitive	(e.g., by thinking, to learn new things)
Etymological	(e.g., making words, words come from other languages)
Mystical	(e.g., magic)
Social necessity	(e.g., easier than drawing; to write someone far away)

FIGURE 1.3 Response Interpretations for the Literacy Interview.

expression), a unitarian perspective (functional literacy), or a literacy skills perspective (school skills void of concern about knowledge content).

■ *Cognitive development (CD)* stresses literacy as problem solving and the intellectual development that results from interactions between readers and writers.

■ *Emancipatory (E)* perspective views literacy as a vehicle through which social and political change can occur.

■ *Social interaction (SI)* refers to the use of literacy to maintain or establish contact with people.

■ *Romantic ideology (R)* emphasizes readers' construction of their own meaning of text within a student-centered learning environment, as well as individual autonomy.

Question 5 tries to tap into students' understanding of the social need for literacy from an historical perspective. Students' example responses are provided on the response sheet (Figure 1.3). The responses, especially if they cluster into one or two response types, provide teachers with insights into their students' perspectives on the purposes for reading and writing as well as how teachers may need to modify their instructional practices to help students understand that literacy is used for multiple purposes.

MAKING INSTRUCTIONAL DECISIONS

When instructional decisions are based on one data source or assessment tool, inappropriate placement of students in special needs settings or the use of inappropriate materials may result. Quality instructional decisions result from a variety of data sources. Classroom teachers and reading specialists understand the need to use more than one assessment tool for instructional decision making. "When a conclusion is supported by data collected from a number of different instruments, its validity is thereby enhanced" (Fraenkel & Wallen, 1993, p. 400).

The assessment tools we present and others described in professional literature are only useful if they help teachers make sound instructional decisions. For example, often included in interest inventories are questions such as "What is your favorite color?" or "Who lives with you at your house?" The first question may be an "ice breaker," included to make a student feel at ease during an interview. However, a student's response of "blue" is not really going to help a teacher plan for the student's instruction. The second question may be considered intrusive unless the information is needed to make parental or caregiver contacts. This information is usually available in other ways such as school admission cards.

A rule of thumb that we keep in mind when deciding what questions to ask students is this: What will I do with the answer? If the answer is going to make your instruction more appropriate for the student, then ask the question. If it doesn't, then don't ask.

References

Drummond, M. J. (1994). *Learning to see: Assessment through observation.* York, ME: Stenhouse Publishing.

FairTest: The National Center for Fair & Open Testing. (n.d.). The limits of standardized tests for diagnosing and assisting student learning. Retrieved June 15, 2004, from www.FairTest.org

Fraenkel, J., & Wallen, N. (1993). *How to design and evaluate research in education.* New York: McGraw-Hill.

Meyerson, M. J. (1997). *Helping students explore the emancipatory nature of literacy.* Paper presented at the National Council of Teachers of English, Detroit, MI.

Walmsley, S. (1991). Literacy in the elementary classroom. In E. Jennings & A. Purves (Eds.), *Literate systems and individual lives: Perspectives on literacy and schooling.* Albany, NY: State University of New York Press.

PART II

When Struggling Readers and Writers Need to Improve Interest, Attitude, and Motivation

Before we begin implementing our strategies for improved word recognition, comprehension, and fluency, we believe that it is essential to first address struggling readers' affective needs as they relate to motivation as well as what teachers can do to enhance student motivation. Struggling readers often sit in classrooms where they have probably not had much opportunity to feel successful in literacy. They sit among proficient readers who rapidly recognize words, read aloud with smooth and fluent expression, and participate in book discussions. Struggling readers are frequently presented with teacher-selected materials, either grade-level selections that are too difficult for them or below-grade level materials in which they have no interest.

While teachers hope that children will be intrinsically motivated to engage in literacy, we need to demonstrate to struggling readers how to be self-motivated through the incorporation of choice, control, challenge, and purpose into the daily classroom routines (Ames, 1992; Gambrell, 1996; Oldfather, 1993; Pintrich & Schunk, 1996; Turner & Paris, 1995). Figure 2.1 shows the interrelationship between the components of motivation. Teachers who are mindful of these interrelationships will help struggling readers be successful through explicit instruction in how to choose reading materials for specific purposes and thus give students control and appropriate challenge over their own reading.

The classroom climate is an important element to consider for nurturing students' motivation to read and write. If you have ever watched youngsters as they play video games, you will notice that they seem to be in another world as they engage in the fast action of the latest video craze. In a real sense they *are* in another world; they have entered a state of total concentration and are one with the game. These optimal

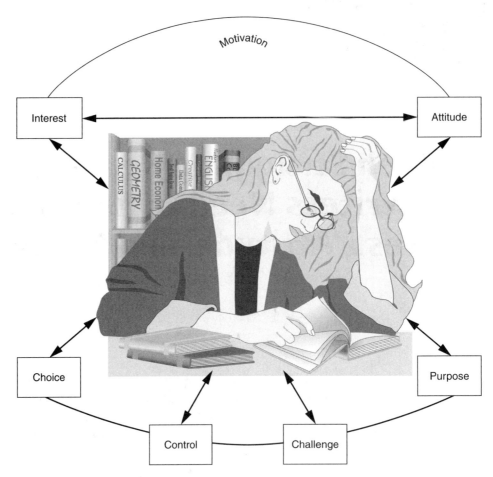

FIGURE 2.1 Components of Motivation.

experiences (Csikszentmihalyi, 1990) can happen to everyone when we are engaged in meaningful activities and enter a state of "flow."

Flow tends to happen when a person faces a clear set of goals that requires appropriate responses. It is easy to enter flow in games such as chess, tennis, or poker because they have goals and rules for action that make it possible for the player to act without questioning what should be done, and how (Csikszentmihalyi, 1997, p. 29). Avid readers often experience flow; they literally get lost in a book (Nell, 1988). They become part of the story and lose track of the world around them. Writers, artists, and athletes also describe this pleasurable state of being. The activities may be challenging and difficult, but individuals continue to engage in them to experience the flow.

Classrooms that promote flow are child-centered. Teachers design classroom environments so that children are free to engage in activities of interest to them. For struggling readers, interaction with print that sustains their interests is paramount. So, too, is the time given to pursue interests. In order for flow to occur in the classroom, children must be given the time to enter this state.

Teachers can create a classroom climate that promotes flow by:

1. Establishing a classroom environment that is child-centered. Provide children the opportunity to make choices whenever possible—choice in what to read and write and choice in method of response.

2. Providing classroom time to engage in activities that require students to concentrate and focus. Sustained silent reading and readers/writers workshop are two teaching practices that will help children get in the flow if they are regularly used. Research projects that require children to read reference materials, use the Internet, or study maps also are excellent opportunities for flow. Allow classroom time for projects instead of assigning them for homework.

3. Minimizing interruptions. Keep track of the number of times children interrupt each other as well as how often you interrupt them. If interruptions are excessive, modify your procedures.

THE GOLDILOCKS PLAN

Choice in literacy activities is a component of reading motivation (Gambrell, 1996; Guthrie & Wigfield, 1997; Oldfather, 1993; Sweet & Guthrie, 1996). Several decades ago, Veatch (1959) suggested that students should self-select reading materials and stressed the importance of teaching selection strategies. The Goldilocks Plan for selecting books was outlined by Ohlhausen and Jepsen (1992). Students are taught, in a series of mini-lessons and individual conferences, how to classify their book selections as too hard, too easy, or just right. A book that was too hard was described as one that the student really wanted to read but knew was too difficult at the time. A book that was just right was one that the student wanted to read and could read, while finding only one or two unknown words per page. A book that was too easy was an old favorite, read many times before.

The Power of the Goldilocks Plan for Struggling Readers

Struggling readers select books that are too difficult for a variety of reasons: (a) the books are about a topic in which they are interested; (b) the books are widely read by their peers, and they want to be part of the reading club; and (c) selection strategies have not been discussed with them. The latter is also one of the reasons that they select books that are too easy, along with the fact that these books provide a comfortable and successful experience. Providing struggling readers with the Goldilocks Plan allows them to:

- Feel confident in their ability to read their self-selected books
- Improve their skills through increased reading experiences
- Read a wider variety of texts

Steps to Follow

1. Introduce the concept of too hard, too easy, and just right books.
2. Model using your own books, showing examples of books that are too hard, too easy, and just right for you to read.
3. Have the students spend time exploring each of these categories of books for themselves.
4. In the classroom library, post the questions the students should ask themselves when selecting books using the Goldilocks Plan.

A book is too hard if you answer "yes" to these questions:

1. Are there more than two words on a page you don't know?
2. Are you confused about what is happening in most of this book?
3. When you read, does it sound pretty choppy?
4. Is everyone else too busy and unable to help you?

A book is too easy if you answer "yes" to these questions:

1. Have you read it many, many times before?
2. Do you understand the story very, very well?
3. Do you know (understand, pronounce) almost every word?
4. Can you read it smoothly?

A book is just right if you answer "yes" to these questions:

1. Is this book new to you?
2. Do you understand some of this book?
3. Are there just one or two words per page that you don't know?

Using the Goldilocks Plan with English Language Learners

Diaz-Rico (2004) promoted the necessity of learner autonomy for English language learners. As she stated, "In the final analysis, however, second-language proficiency is an individual achievement. One can *teach* the learner a second language—but only the learner can *learn* it" (p. 104). For students to have autonomy, they need to be provided with opportunities to practice self-management and build self-efficacy. Krashen (1996) noted that although free voluntary reading is an effective bridge from low level to higher level reading, it is one of the pieces most often missing from students' lives. The Goldilocks Plan equips ELL students with a strategy for selecting books to be read during independent reading time.

Using the Goldilocks Plan to Improve Writing

Just as important as students selecting their own reading materials is the need for them to select their own writing topics. The premise of the

Goldilocks Plan can be adapted to students' writing topics. Students can learn to self-question themselves about a topic they are considering for writing. For example:

This writing topic is too hard if you answer "yes" to these questions (unless the purpose is for research, and you will have ample time to explore resources before you begin writing):

1. Is the topic about a place you have never visited?
2. Is it about something you've never experienced?
3. Are there only one or two things that you can think of for your prewriting web?

The writing topic is too easy if you answer "yes" to these questions:

1. Is this a topic you have already written about, edited, and shared several times before?
2. Are you planning to only write "I like it," or "I like it because . . . "?
3. Will your audience remember that you have shared a similar piece before?

The writing topic is just right if you answer "yes" to these questions.

1. Is the topic about a place you have actually visited?
2. Is the topic about something you have actually done yourself?
3. Is the topic something you know really well and want to share your knowledge or experiences about with your audience?

Application and Examples

Introduce the Goldilocks Plan with a read-aloud of a familiar version of *Goldilocks and the Three Bears*. Continue to reinforce the use of the Goldilocks Plan during small group or individual conferences. Encourage students to discuss their recent selections, and the strategies they used for choosing them, with you and with their peers. Make an audiotape of an alternative Goldilocks story, for example, *The Dumb Bunnies*, *Goldilocks and the Three Hares*, or *Somebody and the Three Blairs*. At the end of the tape, once again remind the students of the Goldilocks Plan; have them write about one of their recent selections and how it fit the criteria. Put the tape at a listening center with multiple copies of the book.

Teaching Aids and References for the Goldilocks Plan

Once you have introduced the Goldilocks Plan to students, periodic checks with those children who tend to have difficulty choosing their books may still be necessary. A chart such as the one presented in Forms

2A to 2D in the Appendix can be reproduced and posted in the classroom to help remind children of how to select books.

Professional References

Ames, C. (1992). Classrooms: Goals, structures, and student motivation. *Journal of Educational Psychology, 84*(3), 261–271.

Csikszentmihalyi, M. (1990). *Flow: The psychology of optimal experiences.* New York: Harper & Row.

Csikszentmihalyi, M. (1997). *Finding flow; The psychology of engagement with everyday life.* New York: Basic Books.

Diaz-Rico, L. T. (2004). *Teaching English learners: Strategies and methods.* Boston, MA: Pearson.

Gambrell, L. B. (1996). Creating classroom cultures that foster reading motivation. *The Reading Teacher, 50*(1), 14–25.

Guthrie, J. T., & Wigfield, A. (Eds.). (1997). *Reading engagement: Motivating readers through integrated instruction.* Newark, DE: IRA.

Krashen, S. (1997). Every person a reader. In C. Weaver (Ed.), *Reconsidering a balanced approach to reading* (pp. 425–452). Urbana, IL: National Council of Teachers of English.

Krashen, S. (1996). *Every Person a Reader: An Alternative to the California Task Force Report on Reading.* Burlingame, CA: Language Education Associates.

Nell, V. (1988). *Lost in a book: The psychology of reading for pleasure.* New Haven, CT: Yale University Press.

Ohlhausen, M. M., & Jepsen, M. (1992). Lessons from Goldilocks: "Somebody's been choosing my books but I can make my own choices now!" *The New Advocate, 5,* 31–46.

Oldfather, P. (1993). What students say about motivating experiences in a whole language classroom. *The Reading Teacher, 46*(8), 672–681.

Pintrich, P. R., & Schunk, D. H. (1996). *Motivation in education: Theory, research, and applications.* Englewood Cliffs, NJ: Prentice Hall.

Sweet, A. P., & Guthrie, J. T. (1996). How children's motivations relate to literacy development and instruction. *The Reading Teacher, 49*(8), 660–662.

Turner, J., & Paris, S. G. (1995). How literacy tasks influence children's motivation for literacy. *The Reading Teacher, 48*(8), 662–673.

Veatch, J. (1959). *Individualizing your reading program.* New York: G. P. Putnam's Sons.

Children's Book References

Denim, S. (1994). *The dumb bunnies.* New York: Scholastic.

Petach, H. (1995). *Goldilocks and the three hares.* New York: Putnam.

Tolhurst, M. (1991). *Somebody and the three Blairs.* New York: Orchard.

TALK, TALK, TALK

Engaged readers are those who are motivated, knowledgeable, strategic, and socially interactive (Baumann & Duffy, 1997). Sharing and communicating with others while constructing and extending the meaning of text provides the social interaction component of reading engagement (Gambrell, 1996). Students should talk, talk, talk about their reading experiences. The Conversational Discussion Group (O'Flahavan, 1989; O'Flahavan & Stein, 1992; O'Flahavan, Stein, Wiencek, & Marks, 1992) provides a structure for students to discuss literature. The teacher's role, once the framework is established, is to present questions that prompt the discussion and then leave the group and let the conversation begin. The teacher is then available as a resource when the students need one.

The Power of Talk, Talk, Talk for Struggling Readers

- One component of the framework for the Conversational Discussion Group is a set of rules for interaction (see Figure 2.2). These rules create a format that allows each student to have equal participation in the discussion.

- The struggling reader, whose voice is often lost in a large group discussion controlled by the teacher, has an opportunity to talk with peers.

- In a small group discussion with a set of rules and a focus for text interpretation, the struggling readers can see themselves on an equal playing field with their peers.

Steps to Follow

1. Make a chart, using student input, listing guidelines for interaction. Some examples are: Everyone gets a chance to talk; Do not interrupt

Guidelines for Interactions	Ways to Interpret Text
Everyone gets a chance to talk	Think about the:
Do not interrupt the speaker	Characters
Pay attention to the speaker	Setting
Stay on the subject	Illustrations
	Point of view

FIGURE 2.2   Chart for Literature Discussion.

the speaker; Pay attention to the speaker; and Stay on the subject (Figure 2.2).

2. Brainstorm with students different ways to interpret text and list these in another column on the chart. They can interpret the text by examining the characters, setting, and illustrations, and the point of view taken by the author.

3. To begin a group's discussion, introduce/review the format as outlined on the chart.

4. Pose three questions, based on the text, to the group. The first question should be designed to activate prior knowledge or personal experiences that connect to the selection. The second question should lead the students into the text, and the third should lead to an extension of it.

5. Leave the group and let the discussion begin. Let the students know that you will be available if they have a question.

6. When the peer discussion is over, return to the group for a debriefing. Revisit the chart during the debriefing to check for guidelines that were followed and interpretation strategies that were used. Discuss what could be done to improve the next discussion.

Using Talk, Talk, Talk with English Language Learners

Hadaway, Vardell, and Young (2002) discussed the importance of integrating children's literature into language arts programs for English language learners. An important component of a literature-based program is response, and that is where peer discussions play a primary role. Book talks provide opportunities for ELL students to become familiar with ways to discuss literature; an additional advantage is that the discussions often provide comprehensible input (Peregoy & Boyle, 2005).

Using Talk, Talk, Talk to Improve Writing

Either in preparation for or following the Talk, Talk, Talk session, students can turn to writing about literary elements. Brown (2001) discussed the use of assigned roles for literature discussions. She described the five roles as follows:

1. Artful Artist uses any form of artwork to symbolize an important idea in the text;

2. Literary Luminary highlights significant passages;

3. Discussion Director prepares questions for the group;

4. Capable Connector makes text-to-text, self, or world connections;

5. Word Wizard explores the text for difficult, uncommon, or fascinating words.

Each of the previous roles may be evolved into a piece of writing that is brought to the Talk, Talk, Talk group. Encourage the students to bring notes for their role to the discussion and then turn them into fully written passages after receiving input and feedback from their peers.

Application and Examples

After creating the chart with the guidelines for interaction and interpretation, introduce the Conversational Discussion Group procedure with a read-aloud. Read Patricia Polacco's *Thunder Cake*. Review the guidelines and then pose the three questions. For example: to activate prior knowledge—"How do you feel when there's a thunderstorm in the distance, and it's coming your way?"; to lead the students into the text— "How did the grandmother's attitude about the storm affect the little girl?"; and to lead to an extension of the text—"What did we learn from this story?"

Teaching Aids and References for Talk, Talk, Talk

A chart can be used for record-keeping of the interpretation strategies used by the students. Note the student, date, and title of selection; and check off the literary elements that were discussed: characters, setting, plot events, point of view, and whether or not illustrations were discussed. If you notice that one of the elements is consistently omitted, conduct a mini-lesson for the group. This will provide assistance in helping struggling readers expand their interpretation repertoire. A chart to meet your needs can easily be prepared in a spreadsheet format or in a table from your word processor. For an example of a chart with an entry, see Figure 2.3.

Date	Title	Character	Setting	Plot Events	Point of View	Illust.
9/7/04	Sabrina, Girl Soccer Player	Described Sabrina as a strong, determined girl	Described the soccer field as in need of repair with holes and bumps	Discussed first three important events in chapters one and two	Mentioned that Sabrina was not telling the story, but her best friend was	Said sketches showed Sabrina wore the number 9 on her jersey and she looked taller than the other players on her team

FIGURE 2.3   Discussion Group—Interpretation Strategies.

Professional References

Baumann, J. F., & Duffy, A. M. (1997). *Engaged reading for pleasure and learning: A report from the National Reading Research Center*. Athens, GA: NRRC.

Brown, M. D. (2001). Literature circles build excitement for books! *Education World*. Retrieved September 11, 2003, from http://www.educationworld.com/searchnew/adv results.jp

Gambrell, L. B. (1996). Creating classroom cultures that foster reading motivation. *The Reading Teacher, 50*(1), 14–25.

Hadaway, N. L., Vardell, S. M., & Young, T. A. (2002). *Literature-based instruction with English language learners, K–12*. Boston, MA: Allyn & Bacon.

O'Flahavan, J. F. (1989). *Second graders' social, intellectual, and affective development in varied group discussions about literature: An exploration of participation structure*. Unpublished doctoral dissertation, University of Illinois, Urbana-Champaign.

O'Flahavan, J. F., & Stein, C. (1992). In search of the teacher's role in peer discussions about literature. *Reading in Virginia, 12,* 34–42.

O'Flahavan, J. F., Stein, C., Wiencek, J., & Marks, T. (1992). *Intellectual development in peer discussions about literature: An exploration of the teacher's role (final report)*. Urbana, IL: National Council of Teachers of English.

Peregoy, S. F., & Boyle, O. F. (2005). *Reading, writing, and learning in ESL: A resource book for K–12 teachers*. Boston, MA: Pearson.

Children's Book References

Polacco, P. (1990). *Thunder cake*. New York: Putnam & Grosset.

BOOK STACKING

Blachowicz and Wimett (1994) reported using this strategy with preservice teachers who in turn used it with elementary and middle school students. A wide array of books is collected by the teacher (at least three per student), and the books are placed in varied stacks on each student chair in the classroom. The students are given time to browse the stacks and then sit by a stack that contains at least one book that they would like to read. This strategy provides choice and fosters social interaction for the students; it also provides information on student interests for the teacher.

The Power of Book Stacking for Struggling Readers

- Book stacking provides a structure that nourishes the motivation to read.

    ▪ Used as an introductory activity, the struggling readers can select books with which they have some familiarity.

    ▪ Struggling readers will be provided with opportunities to:

       1. Demonstrate their reading interests

       2. Feel confident in their ability to read the selection

       3. Have a successful reading experience from the on-set

       4. Participate in a book discussion

Steps to Follow

1. Select a large assortment of books that depict a wide variety of interests, genres, and reading levels. There should be a minimum of three books per student.

2. Place a varied stack of books on each student chair in the classroom.

3. Give the students a browsing time of 15 to 20 minutes.

4. Tell students when they find a book that they would like to read to sit by that stack.

5. Direct students to hold a discussion of selections explaining why they chose a particular book/stack.

6. Make notes of the selections of each student to facilitate gathering reading materials of interest to the students in the future.

Using Book Stacking with English Language Learners

Hadaway, Vardell, and Young (2002) discussed the necessity of providing quality children's literature for ELL students. They recommended all genres be made available for student selection. Their premise is that a well-read and well-informed teacher is the key ingredient to promoting reading in the classroom. Teachers must try to keep abreast of quality children's literature. Your school librarian or a knowledgeable peer who keeps up with the latest children's books are good places to start. Websites for the American Library Association and the Horn Book are great resources. With the comfortable environments provided in local bookstores, browsing with a cappuccino might be the best way to discover titles that would fit with your students.

Using Book Stacking to Improve Writing

As students settle down with a book or stack that has prompted their interest, they can be encouraged to extend their reading activities to writing endeavors. A group of Dottie's students who found a common interest in *The BFG* went on to write new adventures for the Big Friendly Giant. They brainstormed different holidays and school events they

Beginner Books	Familiar Titles	Popular Series
Wordless picture books	Fairy Tales	Bailey School Kids
Dr. Seuss titles	Mother Goose	The Littles
Predictable stories	Frog and Toad	Babysitters Club
Rhyming stories	Amelia Bedelia	Boxcar Children
Leveled books	Horrible Harry	Goosebumps
Popular Favorites	**Informational**	**Just-for-Fun**
Eric Carle	Animals	Jokes
Shel Silverstein	Space	Riddles
Jack Prelutsky	Sports	Scary stories
Roald Dahl	Famous people	Tall tales
Shiloh	How-to books	Legends
Charlotte's Web	Magic School Bus	Fables/Myths

FIGURE 2.4   Suggested Groupings for Book Stacking.

celebrated and then wrote the BFG into stories about them. There was: *The BFG Goes to Open House, The BFG Celebrates Halloween, The BFG Hangs up His Stocking, The BFG Gets a Valentine,* and more. Students who meet at a common stack and discover they have similar interests can then carry those interests over into collaborative writing.

Application and Examples

Following the initial Book Stacking activity, students could pair up or form small groups with others who have similar interests. They could buddy read, trade books, hold book discussions, or investigate new books of interest together. A variation of the activity in which the students make the stacks was reported by Blachowicz and Wimett (1994). The students created stacks of books that they believed would be selected by characters in books and then explained their choices in discussion groups.

Teaching Aids and References for Book Stacking

For all classrooms, select books from a wide range of reading levels. Since the continuum of reading levels in any one classroom ranges over a broad spectrum of five or more levels, it is important to provide something for everyone. Be sure to include books from all genres and try to address a variety of interests. See Figure 2.4 for suggestions.

Professional References

Blachowicz, C. L. Z., & Wimett, C. A. (1994). Response to literature: Models for new teachers. In E. H. Cramer & M. Castle (Eds.), *Fostering the love of reading* (pp. 183–195). Newark, DE: IRA.

Hadaway, N. L., Vardell, S. M., & Young, T. A. (2002). *Literature-based instruction with English language learners, K–12.* Boston, MA: Allyn & Bacon.

Children's Book References

Dahl, R. (1982). *The BFG.* New York: Farrar, Straus and Giroux.

LITERACY AND COMPUTERS

The use of computer clip art can serve as a motivational springboard for a struggling reader or writer. A fifth grader tutored at the University of Nevada, Las Vegas (UNLV) Literacy Development Center read at his grade level but was a very reluctant writer. His tutor introduced him to the idea of using clip art on the Center's computer to recreate the scenes from the book he was reading. Once he discovered this activity, which allowed him to use his visualizations to produce a representation of the setting, his motivation to write the accompanying summary increased dramatically.

The student, who was reading *My Side of the Mountain* with his tutor, would painstakingly recreate a scene as described by the author. Knowing that he would have the opportunity to use the computer also motivated him to read carefully for details of the setting and actions of the plot. After creating the scene to his satisfaction, he would then write a summary of the story to accompany it.

The Power of Literacy and Computers for Struggling Readers

Struggling readers are often as limited in their use of classroom computers as they are in other literacy activities. Their peers are able to use the classroom computer for research, communication, reading, and writing. The struggling reader is often unable to conduct research on the computer because the accessed information is written at or above grade level. The struggling reader, who is often a struggling writer, requires constant monitoring or assistance in composing an electronic communication, as well as reading back any received response. Using clip art to represent responses to literature:

- Provides a format for the student to work independently on the computer
- Connects reading and writing
- Provides a motivational spark

Steps to Follow

1. Preview the available clip art and application features on your classroom computer.

2. Provide time for the struggling readers to become familiar with this computer function.

3. Read a book with your students and then model the creation of illustrations of the setting and characters using a clip art program. Complete the process by composing with them a few sentences that accompany the illustrations, while summarizing the storyline of the book.

4. Monitor struggling readers as they complete the same process with a book read either independently or in a guided reading lesson.

5. Add this computer component to the repertoire of motivational strategies available for use by your struggling readers.

Using Literacy and Computers with English Language Learners

The clip art activity fits well with other strategies we use with students who are learning English, along with all other curriculum areas. It is common for teachers of ELL students to show posters or pictures of things they want to make more meaningful for their students. Realia is often present in an ELL classroom. If you are reading a story that mentions a pomegranate, then bring a pomegranate into the classroom. If a picture is worth a thousand words, imagine what the "real thing" must be worth. Whether you have an artistic side yourself or not, you will often find yourself drawing pictures on your whiteboard, even if stick figures is the best you can do, to make something real for your ELL students. The use of the clip art activity is one more strategy to help increase the understanding, vocabulary, and motivation of your English language learners.

Using Literacy and Computers to Improve Writing

As with the boy who used clip art at UNLV's Literacy Development Center, the extension of writing comes naturally after using clip art to create a scene from a book. Students will soon pay more attention to details in the passages of the book so they can accurately recreate them in clip art. These details will then lend themselves to more extensive, descriptive, and accurate written summaries of the reading.

We read *The Night I Followed the Dog* by Nina Laden.

The boy used to think that his dog was boring. Then one night he followed him from the dog house into the city. The boy found out that his dog had a very exciting life at night.

FIGURE 2.5   Using Clip Art to Summarize a Story.

Application and Examples

Read *The Night I Followed the Dog* with your struggling readers. Discuss the different settings, characters, and actions. Gather around the computer and together brainstorm the available clip art, selecting ones that could appropriately be used with this book. Using this lesson for modeling the procedure, Dottie and her intermediate reading students created a summary page with clip art from the school's installed programs (see Figure 2.5).

Teaching Aids and References for Literacy and Computers

Many of the books designed for struggling readers, especially those leveled by Reading Recovery levels, are conducive to use for this activity with basic clip art. The characters are often family members or common animals, and the situations are often familiar ones such as birthday parties. As the struggling readers progress through books that provide less picture support, they should be encouraged to return to the text for words and phrases that describe the characters and settings. Have your students collaborate on lists of characters and items in different settings as they revisit passages from the book. As they become familiar with the clip art, they will already be thinking ahead to how they will design their responses to the latest reading selection.

Children's Book References

George, J. C. (1988). *My side of the mountain*. New York: Penguin.
Laden, N. (1994). *The night I followed the dog*. New York: Scholastic.

OTHER MEDIA

There may be other equipment available in the classroom that can motivate struggling readers. Sometimes useful equipment can be borrowed from elsewhere in the school building or brought in from home. Equipment that could be shared throughout a grade level or school might be purchased through fund raising, grant writing, or the school budget itself. The overhead projector, common equipment in almost every classroom, can be used by students instead of being a tool only for use by the teacher. Photography from the teacher's personal camera brought from home or from one purchased for the classroom can be used in a variety of ways by students. The music and art specialists can be called upon to offer their expertise and loan some equipment or supplies for motivational activities. A piece of equipment that could be shared throughout the school would be a karaoke machine that can be integrated with the classroom television set.

The Power of Other Media for Struggling Readers

Unable to complete grade-level work, struggling readers are often given worksheets to take up their time. They work on fill-in-the-blank skill sheets; they match and color beginning sounds, prefixes, synonyms, antonyms, and homonyms.

■ Using some of the other media allows struggling readers to use their creative senses, which may, at the moment, be more highly developed than their literacy skills.

Steps to Follow

1. Give the students markers and transparencies and have them work together or individually to make a web of their prior knowledge and/or their predictions for a book that they are about to read. Let them use transparencies for book responses; drawing or writing the characters, setting, or plot actions; and provide time for the students to share with the class. One of Dottie's third-grade reading students concisely summarized in one sentence a book that he had read and made it a caption for a transparency (Figure 2.6) to share with his class.

2. Use a classroom camera to provide actual photographs taken of or by the students to inspire reading and writing. Take the students for an

Don't Forget Fun

Even if you win or lose, you still get to have fun.

FIGURE 2.6 An Example of a Student-Made Transparency.

environment walk around the school grounds, taking pictures for them to use for research, reading, or writing activities. Take pictures of school personnel and then let your students interview them to write captions or biographies to go along with the photographs. Brainstorm with the students what questions they could ask during their interviews. For a biography, a sample interview questionnaire is included in the Appendix as Form 3.

3. Gather children's books that use different media for illustrations. Ask the art specialist for assistance with materials and methods. Set up centers in your classroom supplied with different art materials with which your students can experiment. Keep the materials on hand for when students are ready to illustrate their own books. Examples of illustrative techniques that could be used for art centers are watercolors, cut paper, collage, pastels, scratchboard, colored pencils, and woodcuts.

4. Borrow several different hand-held instruments from the music department. Try using them with books that have repetitive phrases. Assign an instrument to each character or action that is repeated throughout the story. Each time the word for the character or action is read, the student makes the musical sound with the instrument.

5. Find access to a karaoke machine that can be interfaced with your classroom television set. Let the music begin, with the lyrics running

across the TV screen; see how motivated those struggling readers will be to read the words to the song along with their peers.

Using Other Media with English Language Learners

All of the Other Media strategies are excellent for use with English language learners because they provide hands-on, meaningful activities that are easily linked to literacy. The use of transparencies, photographs, illustration media, musical instruments, and singing allow students to make important connections to other arts. As stated by Goldberg (2004):

> Like all students, children who are learning another language learn in many ways. Children can be visually oriented, kinesthetic, aural, or logico-mathematical thinkers. While it is good pedagogical practice to keep open all venues for students, it is especially important to do so with second language learners who have the additional burden of expressing themselves in a new language. (p. 9)

Using Other Media to Improve Writing

All of the Other Media strategies have a direct connection to writing. The transparencies are for sharing writing: a web, a prediction, or a response to literature. Photographs taken around the school can be used for creative writing by students, who like to make up stories about the places, people, and things in the photos. Having students write biographies of the school staff involves the students in (a) creating a questionnaire, (b) interviewing skills, (c) note-taking skills, and (d) the entire writing process. The illustration media motivates students to complete their own stories so they can create illustrations for student-authored books. The musical instruments can be used in reverse from accompanying books to creating musical rhythms and tempos and then writing lyrics to go with them.

Application and Example

Using photographs taken around the school grounds provides multiple opportunities for collaborative writing. One activity that is very motivating for students is to give small groups sets of pictures taken in and around the school grounds and send them out to find the sources/ locations of the photos. When they return they become engrossed in writing a creative story to match the photos; they love to include (a) the principal; (b) the name of their school; and (c) some posted rules, for example, no rollerblading, no parking, and so forth. When the students finish writing, they share their photos and stories with the other small groups, usually with much laughter and praise.

Teaching Aids and References for Other Media

A number of different art centers for book illustrations can be developed through the school year for students to explore as they are further motivated to read. Start with one illustration technique; for example, watercolors. Share picture books with watercolor illustrations, discussing with your students the impressions given by watercolors. As students become familiar with this technique, introduce a watercolor center for students to illustrate their own stories. After a month-long investigation, move on to another technique and fully explore it through the sharing of picture books. When ready, create a center with those materials for students to add to their illustration repertoires.

Watercolors

For the watercolor center, gather tempera paints from your art teacher, or purchase inexpensive watercolor paints at your local department store. Add brushes, cups of water, and paper. For examples of watercolor illustrations, gather some of the following picture books:

> *Mirette on the Highwire*, written and illustrated by Emily Arnold McCully
>
> *The Patchwork Quilt*, written by Valerie Flournoy, illustrated by Jerry Pinkney
>
> *Strega Nona*, written and illustrated by Tomie de Paola
>
> *Grandfather's Journey*, written and illustrated by Allen Say
>
> *Tuesday*, written and illustrated by David Wiesner
>
> *Cousin Ruth's Tooth*, written by Amy MacDonald, illustrated by Marjorie Priceman
>
> *Peppe the Lamplighter*, written by Elisa Bartone, illustrated by Ted Lewin
>
> *When I Was Young in the Mountains*, written by Cynthia Rylant, illustrated by Diane Goode
>
> *Cecil's Story*, written by George Ella Lyon, illustrated by Peter Catalanotto
>
> *Possum Magic*, written by Mem Fox, illustrated by Julie Vivas
>
> *The Talking Eggs: A Folktale from the American South*, retold by Robert D. San Souci, illustrated by Jerry Pinkney

Cut Paper

For the cut paper center, gather a variety of types of paper available in your school. There can be construction paper, writing paper, tissue paper, and white and colored photocopy paper. Add scissors and glue or rubber cement to complete the center. For examples of cut paper illustrations, gather some of the following picture books:

> *Golem*, written and illustrated by David Wisniewski
>
> *Rain Player*, written and illustrated by David Wisniewski

Elfwyn's Saga: Story and Pictures, written by David Wisniewski, illustrated by Lee Salsbery

The Warrior and the Wise Man, written and illustrated by David Wisniewski

Harlem, written by Walter Dean Myers, illustrated by Christopher Myers

Saint Valentine, written and illustrated by Robert Sabuda

Once Upon Another, written and illustrated by Suse MacDonald and Bill Oakes

Numblers, written and illustrated by Suse MacDonald and Bill Oakes

Mouse Paint, written and illustrated by Ellen Stoll Walsh

The Emperor and the Kite, written by Jane Yolen, illustrated by Ed Young

Color Zoo, written and illustrated by Lois Ehlert

Chicka Chicka Boom Boom, written by John Archambault and Bill Martin, Jr., illustrated by Lois Ehlert

Fish Eyes: A Book You Can Count On, written and illustrated by Lois Ehlert

Collage

For the collage center, gather a variety of materials. Surprisingly, you may find many of them right in your classroom. Think about materials you've gathered for other projects across the curriculum. There was probably a little bit of this and a little bit of that left over that you didn't want to throw away. Some extra materials can be found by taking a walk around the school grounds. The collage center can include just about anything: paper, fabric, yarn, ribbon, seeds, twigs, pebbles, cottonballs, craft sticks, plastic wrap, bottle caps, broken pencils, and so on. Add glue and scissors to complete the center. For examples of collage illustrations, gather some of the following picture books:

The Very Hungry Caterpillar, written and illustrated by Eric Carle

The Very Quiet Cricket, written and illustrated by Eric Carle

Smoky Night, written by Eve Bunting, illustrated by David Diaz

Peter's Chair, written and illustrated by Ezra Jack Keats

Goggles!, written and illustrated by Ezra Jack Keats

The Snowy Day, written and illustrated by Ezra Jack Keats

Where the Forest Meets the Sea, written and illustrated by Jeannie Baker

Inch by Inch, written and illustrated by Leo Lionni

Arrow to the Sun: A Pueblo Indian Tale, adapted and illustrated by Gerald McDermott

Pastels

The pastels might be available from your art specialist or from your school supplies. If not, they can be purchased at your local arts and crafts store. Otherwise, you can use colored chalk, which is readily available and much less expensive. Add paper for the background and a box of tissues to complete the center. For examples of pastel illustrations, gather some of the following picture books:

Lon Po Po: A Red-Riding Hood Story from China, translated and illustrated by Ed Young

Hoops, written by Robert Burleigh, illustrated by Stephen T. Johnson

While I Sleep, written by Mary Calhoun, illustrated by Ed Young

Whoo-oo Is It?, written by Megan McDonald, illustrated by S. D. Schindler

The Sleepytime Book, written by Jan Wahl, illustrated by Arden Johnson

The Samurai's Daughter: A Japanese Legend, retold by Robert D. San Souci, illustrated by Stephen T. Johnson

Chin Yu Min and the Ginger Cat, written by Jennifer Armstrong, illustrated by Mary Grandpre

Haircuts at Sleepy Sam's, written by Michael R. Strickland, illustrated by Keaf Holliday

Angels in the Dust, written by Margot Theis Raven, illustrated by Roger Essley

Scratchboard

The scratchboard art center can be simply equipped with all colors of crayons and extra black ones. To acquire the effect of the scratchboard technique, the students color a paper and then color over it with black crayon. Almost anything available in the classroom (scissors, a blunt pencil, an opened paper clip, the edge of a ruler, etc.) could then be used to scratch off the black to create a picture. Kits for this activity can be purchased at your local teacher/educator supply store. For examples of scratchboard illustrations, gather some of the following picture books:

The Elephant's Wrestling Match, written by Judy Sierra, illustrated by Brian Pinkney

The Ballad of Belle Dorcas, written by William Hooks, illustrated by Brian Pinkney

Where Does the Trail Lead? written by Burton Albert, illustrated by Brian Pinkney

The Faithful Friend, written by Robert D. San Souci, illustrated by Brian Pinkney

Sukey and the Mermaid, written by Robert D. San Souci, illustrated by Brian Pinkney

The Gettysburg Address, illustrated by Michael McCurdy

Giants in the Land, written by Diana Appelbaum, illustrated by Michael McCurdy

The Beasts of Bethlehem, verse by X. J. Kennedy, illustrated by Michael McCurdy

Duke Ellington, written by Andrea Davis Pinkney, illustrated by Brian Pinkney

Colored Pencils

A variety of colored pencils and white paper is all that is needed for this art center. For examples of colored pencil illustrations, gather some of the following picture books:

Frogs, Toads, Lizards, and Salamanders, written and illustrated by Nancy Winslow Parker and Joan R. Wright

Puss in Boots, written by Charles Perrault, translated by Malcolm Arthur, and illustrated by Fred Marcellino

Fenwick's Suit, written and illustrated by David Small

Song and Dance Man, written by Karen Ackerman, illustrated by Stephen Gammell

Waiting for the Whales, written by Sheryl McFarlane, illustrated by Ron Lightburn

The Cat & The Fiddle & More, written by Jim Aylesworth, illustrated by Richard Hull

Wolf Plays Alone, written and illustrated by Dominic Catalano

We're Making Breakfast for Mother, written by Shirley Neitzel, illustrated by Nancy Winslow Parker

It's Disgusting—And We Ate It!: True Food Facts From Around the World, written by James Solheim, illustrated by Eric Brace

Woodcuts

For the woodcut art center, let the students experiment with the medium, using Styrofoam materials (Laughlin & Watt, 1986). Save those Styrofoam packaging trays from the grocery store, or purchase some plates of that material. Borrow a brayer from your art teacher, or purchase an inexpensive mini-paint roller from your department store. Add India ink or paint, pencils, and construction paper to complete the center. The students draw a picture on the Styrofoam with a pencil, making sure that their marks are deeply indented. Next, they use the roller to cover the picture with paint or India ink. The last step is to put a piece of construction paper over the picture; this will provide a print that is the opposite of the picture drawn on the plate. For examples of woodcut illustrations, gather some of the following picture books:

Drummer Hoff, adapted by Barbara Emberley, illustrated by Ed Emberley

A Story A Story: An African Tale, written and illustrated by Gail E. Haley

Ever Heard of an Aardwolf?, written by Madeline Moser, illustrated by Barry Moser

Swan Sky, written and illustrated by Keizaburo Tejima

The Devils Who Learned to Be Good, written and illustrated by Michael McCurdy

Antler, Bear, Canoe: A Northwoods Alphabet Year, written and illustrated by Betsy Bowen

The Dancing Palm Tree, and Other Nigerian Folktales, written by Barbara K. Walker, illustrated by Helen Siegl

Bayberry Bluff, written and illustrated by Blair Lent

Teaching Aids and References for Other Media

Goldberg, M. (2004). *Teaching English language learners through the arts: A SUAVE experience*. Boston, MA: Pearson.

Laughlin, M. K., & Watt, L. S. (1986). *Developing learning skills through children's literature: An idea book for K–5 classrooms and libraries*. Phoenix, AZ: Oryx Press.

Using Computers for Writing in Middle School

Students of all ages struggle with writing. Some have difficulty with handwriting, while others lack spelling skills. For those reasons, Cecil and Gipe (2003) discussed using computers, which have several advantages, for writing in middle school. They noted computers can be used throughout the writing process:

1. In prewriting, the Internet can be used to investigate a topic. While brainstorming, they can use the word processor to make webs, clusters, or lists of related ideas.

2. The rough draft may be typed without the worry of erasures for misspelled words and poor indecipherable handwriting.

3. In the revising and editing stages, deletions can be made, sentences or phrases can easily be moved, and the spellcheck and Thesaurus can be referred to for accuracy.

4. For the stage of publishing, struggling writers can produce a polished final copy to share with others.

Professional References

Cecil, N. L., & Gipe, J. P. (2003). *Literacy in the intermediate grades: Best practices for a comprehensive program*. Scottsdale, AZ: Holcomb Hathaway, Publishers.

ASSESSING INTEREST, ATTITUDE, AND MOTIVATION

Assessing students' affective reading development can be done with observations, checklists, conferences, interviews, or surveys. As mentioned earlier in this chapter, observation provides details of a student's literacy behaviors. However, interpretations and implications must be made with care. If a student cannot settle down with a book during independent reading time, you should not conclude that the student lacks motivation or interest. There may be several other reasons contributing to this behavior.

A list of recent reading choices made by students can provide valuable information about their reading interests. A brief conference with a student, with only a few questions about reading interests, will furnish important information for the teacher. You can gain insight into the reading interests of students, and appropriate reading materials can be provided.

There are numerous published interview protocols and surveys aimed at determining children's interest, attitude, and/or motivation. Many of the surveys use Likert scale responses and ask children to respond to items such as: "I like to read at home," and "I feel proud when I read a book." The Elementary Reading Attitude Survey (McKenna & Kear, 1990) is a widely used instrument that features four different Garfield expressions, ranging from happiest to very upset, to assess younger children's attitudes about reading. This survey is particularly informative because it provides two scores—an academic and a recreation reading score—which allows classroom teachers to understand a child's perspectives and feeling about reading both in and out of school.

The MRP—Motivation to Read Profile (Gambrell, Palmer, Codling, & Mazzoni, 1996) assesses a student's self-concept as a reader and the student's value of reading. It may be used to determine motivation of students in grades 2–6. MRP consists of two parts: a reading survey that children complete independently; and a conversational interview which is completed one-on-one with a child. The survey consists of 20 multiple choice questions that focus on children's self-perception as readers, the strategies they use when reading, and how students perceive others and view them as readers. In the conversational interview, you engage a student in a "natural conversation" about fiction and nonfiction books and general reading interests such as "tell me about your favorite author" and "how do you find out about books?"

Both these instruments were published in *The Reading Teacher* and may be copied for classroom use.

Professional References

Gambrell, L. B., Palmer, B. M., Codling, R. M., & Mazzoni, S. A. (1996). Assessing motivation to read. *The Reading Teacher*, *49*, 518–533.

McKenna, M. C., & Kear, D. J. (1990). Measuring attitudes toward reading: A new tool for teachers. *The Reading Teacher*, *43*(9) 626–639.

PART III

When Struggling Readers and Writers Need to Improve Word Recognition

Word recognition, the ability to identify words through decoding, sight, context, configuration, or by other means, is one of the main components of literacy, as well as one of the areas that causes difficulty for struggling readers. As a classroom teacher or reading specialist, you are well aware that all students at some time have difficulty recognizing some words. Struggling readers, however, often have a very limited sight vocabulary (words instantly recognized), over rely on one recognition strategy (e.g., phonics), and/or fail to understand that meaning is inherent in the reading process, and therefore inaccurately word call (e.g., "house" for "horse").

Gipe (1995) suggests that there are three types of word recognition difficulties related to instructional practices: (a) too much instruction in word recognition, (b) too little instruction in word recognition, and (c) unbalanced instruction in word recognition in that one strategy is emphasized over another. When we consider the big picture of literacy instruction, the notion of balance rings through all reasons for good instructional practices. The strategies presented here are included because they easily provide balanced instructional practice for students and incorporate reading, writing, listening, and speaking.

Reference

Gipe, J. (1995). *Corrective reading techniques for the classroom teacher*. Scottsdale, AZ: Gorsuch Scarisbrick Publishers.

LANGUAGE EXPERIENCE APPROACH

While most references to the language experience approach (LEA) (Allen, 1976; Coate & Castle, 1989; Hall, 1978) include in their definitions use with young students, it can also be used successfully with older students in grades 3 through 8 who are struggling with learning to read, as well as with second language learners (Barr & Johnson, 1997). Struggling readers, regardless of age, have many life experiences that teachers can tap into to create text. It is important to recognize that some second language learners or students of poverty may have experiences that differ from your experiences or that they may offer different perspectives on the same experience. For example, a fifth-grade teacher who took a group of inner city students to another part of town to visit an art museum was amazed that most of the after-the-field-trip discussion centered on the bus ride across town and the sights seen from the bus window rather than the art in the museum. The students had seen many paintings when the museum sent a traveling show to their school the previous year. The bus ride was the new experience that the teacher could capitalize on for a language experience story.

If a broad definition of LEA is employed, then the multitude of classroom experiences provided through a student-centered, "hands-on" curriculum is fertile ground for language experience "stories," as well as the clarification of new concepts. Science and mathematics, in particular, provide students with new vocabulary and concepts that can be integrated into the LEA (Heller, 1988).

LEA can be used with individual students as well as with small groups. From a social constructivist perspective (Newman & Holzman, 1993), LEA can be very successful when students work together with a "more knowledgeable other." This person may be the teacher, a more experienced student, teacher aide, or parent.

The Power of the Language Experience Approach for Struggling Readers

The language experience approach as it relates to word recognition makes available an instructional framework for teaching struggling readers. LEA provides:

- A way to reinforce the one-to-one correspondence between spoken and written language
- A meaningful context based on students' knowledge and experience
- The use of repeated readings of the same text as well as repetition of high-frequency words
- A meaning context to examine components of language (words, phonemes, and morphemes)
- The modeling of sentence structure by the teacher

Steps to Follow

1. Focus on an experience that is either common to all students from outside their school experiences (e.g., going to the grocery store) or an experience that is the result of a class trip, class lesson, or activity.

2. Generate vocabulary that authors most likely would use if they were writing about the topic or idea.

3. Record students' dictation. This may be done on chart paper or using an overhead projector. Make sure students can clearly see what you write. You can also incorporate the use of the computer with a projection system (Labbo, Eakle, & Montero, 2003). With young students, try not to rephrase students' sentences unless grammatical errors make the text meaning confusing. With older students and adults, editing makes more sense.

4. Read the text aloud, modeling fluency and making connections between speech and print by pointing to each word.

5. Invite students to read and reread the text orally and silently. This promotes fluency.

6. Once the complete text is known by the student or group, begin to focus on the smaller components of the text such as sentences, words, and letters. This will foster word recognition skills. Use sentence strips and word cards so students can manipulate the text.

Using the Language Experience Approach with English Language Learners

Students who are learning English bring with them an understanding of their native language structure. With very young students, this knowledge may only be oral; older students who have attended schools in another country bring both oral and written language knowledge. Through LEA you model how the syntactical structure of English may differ or be the same as students' native language. For example, in Spanish, the adjective is placed after the noun; in English, the adjective is placed before the noun.

Spanish Structure:	Ia manzana rojo
Literal Translation:	the apple red
English Structure:	the red apple

Thus, while an experience visiting the local grocery store may result in identifying different fruits (apples, oranges, bananas, etc.) and learning the English words for each in isolation, LEA demonstrates how English is written so that isolated words become part of a meaning-making experience.

Using the Language Experience Approach to Improve Writing

As you write students' dictated sentences in LEA, you are modeling components of the writing process. When students provide complete thoughts and ideas, you can model syntactical structure and writing conventions (capitalization, punctuation, etc.). When their ideas are not fully formed, you can help them expand their thoughts by asking questions (What can you add to that idea?) and invite collaboration (What can someone else add to this idea?). Depending on the students' instructional needs, you may also model how to spell words through sound/symbol correspondence, analogy, or structural analysis.

Encourage students to follow your lead when writing independently by asking themselves questions as they write. You may want to post a list of "Writers' Questions" in the classroom and remind students to refer to them when writing independently or collaboratively.

Application and Examples

The LEA can be used with an activity as easy to do as playing "Here We Go Round the Mulberry Bush" right in the classroom. Dottie played this game and then read a book by the same title with some of her English language learner reading students. Following that activity, the students dictated some new verses, which Dottie printed out on the computer. Each new verse was centered at the bottom of a single page for the students to illustrate and reread. One of the verses was, "This is the way we dance around, dance around, dance around." A few days later in a lesson with a new book, one of the girls, a preprimer reader in English, proudly recognized the word *dance* when she came across it in the text.

Another example comes from a story dictated to his tutor by a student who attended the Literacy Development Center at the University of Nevada, Las Vegas. Sammy is a second grader who was practically a "nonreader." He knew fewer than 20 sight words and possessed some knowledge of sound/symbol correspondence. He was able, according to his tutor, "to talk up a storm." Sammy and his tutor took a walk through the desert garden on campus. Then Sammy dictated the following:

> We walked to the desert garden today to see all the plants. I never knew there were so many different plants. I liked the teddy bear cactus the best. You have to be careful with cactus because it can stick you and then the sticker stays in your hand. Cactus don't need much water so that's why they grow so big in Las Vegas.

After Sammy dictated the story, the tutor read the story to Sammy, had him echo read with her, and finally read it on his own. Once he seemed secure with the overall text, the tutor asked Sammy to find specific words from the story that were printed on 3 × 5 cards (see Figure 3.1). The tutor selected these words for Sammy based on his previous sight word needs (e.g., "because") and for their interest for

FIGURE 3.1   Word Cards.

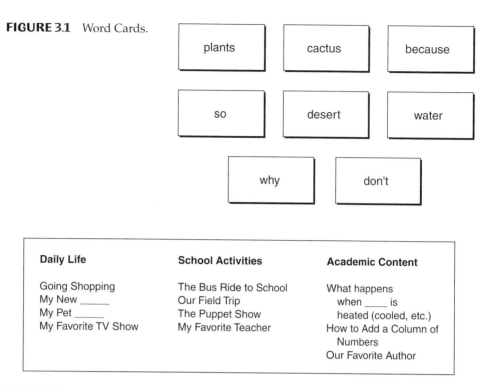

plants	cactus	because
so	desert	water
why	don't	

Daily Life	School Activities	Academic Content
Going Shopping	The Bus Ride to School	What happens
My New _____	Our Field Trip	when ____ is
My Pet _____	The Puppet Show	heated (cooled, etc.)
My Favorite TV Show	My Favorite Teacher	How to Add a Column of
		Numbers
		Our Favorite Author

FIGURE 3.2   Language Experience Approach Topics.

Sammy (e.g., "cactus"). A variety of activities were used to reinforce sight vocabulary: matching words on the card with words in the text, masking words in the text, and writing the words in Sammy's personal dictionary. Sammy kept the story in his portfolio to use it again over several days.

Another word recognition lesson centered on /n/ as in *need*, *never*, and *knew*. "What is special about *knew?*" the tutor asked. This gave the tutor the opportunity to show Sammy the homophones *new* and *knew* and to help Sammy distinguish their use based on word meaning.

Teaching Aids and References for the Language Experience Approach

The best topics for LEA are based on actual experiences that students have had. Keep in mind that topics may come from daily life, school activities, or academic content. Figure 3.2 shows some suggested topics that may be used with groups or with individual students for language experience.

Allen, R. V. (1976). *Language experiences in communication.* Boston: Houghton Mifflin.

Barr, R., & Johnson, B. (1997). *Teaching reading and writing in the elementary classroom.* New York: Longman.

Coate. S., & Castle, M. (1989). Integrating LEA and invented spelling in kindergarten. *The Reading Teacher, 42,* 516–519.

Hall, M. (1978). *The language experience approach for teaching reading: A research perspective.* Newark, DE: International Reading Association.

Heller. M. F. (1988). Comprehending and composing through language experience. *The Reading Teacher, 41,* 130–135.

Labbo, L., Eakle, A. J., & Montero, M. K. (2003). Digital language experience approach: Using digital photographs and software as a language experience approach innovation. (retrieved 7/29/04): http://www.readingonline.org

Newman, F., & Holzman, L. (1993). *Lev Vygotsky*: Revolutionary scientist. London: Routledge.

READING THE ENVIRONMENT

Some struggling readers are unaware of the actual number of words they can read because they often perceive reading only as a school activity. The words around them in their community outside of school can be used to bolster their confidence and broaden their view of the place of reading in the real world. You can assist struggling readers by bringing the students' world outside school into the classroom and thus help students to read the world around them and acknowledge the importance of nonschool print.

The use of environmental print in the classroom was a topic of interest during the 1980s (Bissex, 1980; Taylor, 1983; Teale & Sulzby, 1986). Researchers suggested that teachers could help young readers and writers better understand the connection between oral and written language by bringing print from the real world into the classroom. More recently, Orellana and Hernandez (1999) suggested that literacy walks in urban environments also help teachers to learn more about their students while using environmental print to teach words.

The Power of Reading the Environment for Struggling Readers

Reading the environment helps struggling readers because it:

- Demonstrates the use of print and its importance beyond the classroom.
- Builds self-confidence by showing struggling readers that they know many words even though they may not find the words in the classroom.
- Provides second language learners with concrete examples.
- Utilizes local resources.

Steps to Follow

1. Take students on a walking tour around the school neighborhood and have students write down any words or phrases that they see. If the walking tour is not possible, then take pictures of the community that include store signs, billboards, and street signs.

2. Back in the classroom, have the students create a replica of the community. They can make a mural or a model. Make word and phrase cards for labeling each item.

3. In small groups, have the students write about their community by incorporating the words and phrases into their text.

4. Have all students contribute to the making of a class community dictionary to keep track of new words.

5. Use community newspapers, flyers, and advertisements to expand word recognition.

Using Reading the Environment with English Language Learners

Since reading the environment focuses on the use of text outside of school, you can encourage ELL students to notice all forms of text including signs written in their native language. This also helps students value their language because they see it as an acceptable response to a school activity.

Text in the form of international signs and symbols can also help students learn new words. For example, when some students see the symbol below, they may say it means that "no smoking" is allowed in a particular place. Other students may comment that the symbol means "smoking is prohibited" in a place. Both interpretations are correct but the meaning is expressed differently, thus helping ELL students, as well as English-only students, to learn new words in meaningful contexts.

Using Reading the Environment to Improve Writing

Once students have gathered words from the local environment you can encourage them to write about topics they may not have considered before. For example, after a walk to a local food market, students may take note of words in the environment such as *produce, meat, express lane, dairy products, customer service*, and *store manager*. After discussing the meaning of the individual words and phrases, you can encourage students to write about their experiences at the food market, create a short play about returning some meat to customer service, or a humorous story about the "slow" express lane.

American Express Cards	Now Open in the Sidewalk Cafe
One Way	Do Not Enter
No Smoking	Box Office
Judy Bayley Theatre	Artemus W. Ham Concert Hall
Department of Theatre Arts	Emergency Phone
Performing Arts Center Office	Automatic Door
Pull	Power Assist
Caution	KLVX TV Welcomes You
Before You Write a Check Read This!	No Refunds
Stairs	Mastercard
VISA	The Canadian Brass
Tickets Now on Sale	Reserved Parking
Tow Away Zone	UNLV
No Carts or Vehicles Beyond This Point	Fire Lane
Burger King Express	Pizza Hut Express

FIGURE 3.3   Words from a Walking Tour to the Music Hall.

A —Apply within	E —
	F —Flamingo Avenue
B —Bingo Sunday Night	G —Grill and Restaurant
C —Community Center	H —Hospital Zone
D —Donuts	I —Interstate 95

FIGURE 3.4   Classroom Community Dictionary.

Application and Example

The Paradise Professional Development School (PPDS) is located on the campus of the University of Nevada, Las Vegas, right in the middle of an urban area. It is not an affluent school by any means; over 70% of the students receive free or reduced lunches. In addition, 40% of the students have a language other than English as their first language.

Dottie was the remedial reading teacher for grades 3, 4, and 5 at the PPDS. She took advantage of the school's location by taking her students on walking tours to read the environment. One place the students like to visit is the box office of the music hall. Students were given some 3 × 5 cards and a pencil. When they found words of interest to them or words they knew, the students were instructed to write them down on the cards.

When they returned to Dottie's room, the word cards were gathered and compiled into a list, which Dottie made into a poster for the students to see (Figure 3.3). After reading the words and phrases several times together, the students began to suggest word categories. For example, the students thought of one group as the "No Words": *no smoking*, *no carts or vehicles beyond this point*, and *no refunds*. Other words were related to safety: *caution*, *fire lane*, and *emergency phone*.

Teaching Aids and References for Reading the Environment

Figure 3.4 shows the beginnings of a classroom community dictionary.

Bissex, G. (1980). *Gnys at wrk: A child learns to read and write*. Cambridge, MA: Harvard University Press.

Orellana, M., & Hernandez, A. (1999). Talking the walk: Children reading urban environmental print. *The Reading Teacher, 52*, 612–619.

Taylor, D. (1983). *Family literacy: Young children learning to read and write*. Exeter, NH: Heinemann.

Teale, W., & Sulzby, E. (Eds.). (1986). *Emergent literacy: Writing and reading*. Norwood, NJ: Ablex.

DECODING BY ANALOGY

Balanced literacy instruction implies instruction in the three levels: comprehension, production, and metalinguistic awareness. Comprehension refers to the understanding of spoken or written language. Production is the creation of oral or written language. Metalinguistic awareness is an individual's ability to distance oneself from the comprehension and production of language and focus on the components of language itself. A student who is able to rhyme, spell, and edit is metalinguistically aware.

Metalinguistic awareness is the most abstract level of language and thus requires that students reach a level of abstract thinking. It is for this reason that young students in the primary grades may not be successful with some instructional practices, such as phonics. Unfortunately, many standardized reading tests for the early grades tend to question students on their abilities to manipulate language rather than the comprehension and production of it. Some students are labeled as remedial readers based on test results that require a level of thinking that students do not all reach at the same time.

The area of metalinguistic awareness that has received the most attention recently is phonemic awareness, the ability to understand that spoken language is made up of individual sounds—phonemes. A student who correctly answers the question, "With what sound does *bat* begin?" is phonemically aware. A student who produces a response such as "flies" or "ball" is trying to make sense of the question (comprehend) and is focused on the meaning of the word (i.e., a mammal that flies or a piece of sports equipment used to hit a ball). Responses such as these indicate that a student has not reached the phonemic awareness level and may not be developmentally ready for formal phonics instruction.

This, then, becomes the great dilemma for teachers: If students have not entered into the metalinguistic/phonemic awareness stage of language development and yet they are tested on this, how can I help them become successful readers?

One successful strategy for struggling readers is the decoding by analogy (Cunningham, 1995). Gaskins and colleagues (1992, 1997) described the success of this method used at the Benchmark School, a school especially designed for students who struggle with reading. The strategy is based on what mature readers do when they encounter an unknown word in text. Students learn to identify key phonograms (for example, -*at*; -*ump*; and -*ight*) and then use what is known to decode the unknown. Wang and Gaffney (1998) showed that first graders were able to read more words correctly when shown the decoding by analogy methods.

The Power of Decoding by Analogy for Struggling Readers

- Decoding by analogy gives struggling readers a real boost because they can quickly increase their reading vocabulary.
- The strategy allows the reader to focus on letter groups and their corresponding sound rather than a letter-by-letter/sound-by-sound decoding process.
- Students learn to decode multisyllabic words easily once basic phonograms are learned.

Steps to Follow

1. This process assumes that students know the basic sound/symbol correspondence for consonants, blends, and digraphs.
2. Begin with a simple phonogram that is a known sight word, such as "at" in *cat*.
3. Teach students this phrase, which will help them form the analogy: If this is—, then this must be—. For example, "If this is *cat*, then this must be *bat*," where *cat* is the known word and *bat* is the new word.
4. Post phonograms in the classroom on a bulletin board or "word wall" for a quick reference when students are reading and writing.
5. Find authentic texts for students to use to practice their skills in decoding by analogy. Avoid texts that overuse phonograms, however, so that students apply their skill in real reading situations. Text, such as "The fat cat sat on a mat," are of no real value to students.

Using Decoding by Analogy with English Language Learners

Decoding by analogy requires students to be at the metalinguistic stage of language development. When students first learn English, the focus of instruction should be on making meaning. Once they know simple sight words and are ready for more abstract components of language, introduce ELL students to decoding by analogy as described step-by-step.

Using Decoding by Analogy to Improve Writing

"I don't know how to spell it" is a statement common in the classroom when students are trying to write. While there are many high-frequency words with irregular spelling patterns, there are also many words that do conform to predictable patterns that students can learn to spell through a similar decoding by analogy strategy. When students are more confident with their spelling, they will often become more fluent in writing their thoughts and ideas.

Because decoding by analogy requires students to be able to identify the onset and rime of unknown words, the reverse or recoding by analogy may be employed to help writing fluency. Teach students the following phrase:

If I can spell—, then I can spell—.

As they are writing, students may try this approach before asking for assistance. For example, to spell *flight*, have students think of a word that belongs to the same word family posted on a word wall such as *right*. Then by applying the spelling phrase, the unknown word may be easily revealed:

If I can spell *right*: *r-ight*, then I can spell *flight*: *fl-ight*.

It is important for students to remember the rime as a chunk of letters that belong together rather than individual letters.

Application and Example

Brandon is a third grader who attended the Literacy Development Center for tutoring. His oral reading was very laborious; he seemed to be very confused when confronted with words that were multisyllabic and broke down to a letter-by-letter decoding. He also was very reluctant to try new words. He was aware of the fact that he was falling behind his classmates in school. During the initial interview, Brandon told his tutor Steve that he wanted to learn how to read "really big words."

Results from initial assessments showed that Brandon knew most high-frequency words, initial and final consonant sounds, two-letter blends, and short vowels. Steve decided to try to help Brandon apply what he already knew to decode unfamiliar words.

Steve: There are lots of ways to figure out big words. I'm going to show you a way that you can use because you already know many things about words. Let's look at this word: *ligament*. Do you know what it is?

Brandon: No.

Steve: Okay, let's look at the first three letters, *lig*. The *l* is a consonant, the *i* is a vowel, and the *g* is a consonant. Do you know another word that looks like *lig* that has a different first consonant but the same *i* and *g*? It would look like _____*ig*.

Brandon: No.

Steve: Sure you do. What about *b-i-g*?

Brandon: That's *big*.

Steve: And *p-i-g*?

Brandon: That's *pig*.

Steve: So how would you say *l-i-g*?

Brandon: *Lig*.

Steve: Okay, so the first part of the word is *lig* and we know that because we know similar words like *big* and *pig*. Now let's look at the rest of the word: *a-ment*. I'm going to tell you that the *a* is a short *a* sound, so now we have *lig-a*. Look at the last part, *ment*. Do you know any word that looks like that—that has a different first consonant instead of the *m* but the same other letters *ent*?

Brandon: I know *went*.

Steve: Great! So if *w-e-n-t* is *went*, then *m-e-n-t* is. . . .

Brandon: *ment*.

Steve: Right. Now let's put it all together.

Brandon: *lig-a-ment*.

Steve: And if we say it fast it's *ligament*. Do you know what a ligament is?

Brandon: No.

Steve: Let's read this sentence with the word and see if you can tell what it means.

Brandon: The football player tore a ligament in his leg.

Steve: What do you think a ligament is?

Brandon: Is it a muscle?

Steve: Yes, it is part of our body that connects muscles. If you tear a ligament, it can be very painful. Now, let's see if you can try another word using this strategy.

am	clam, ham, jam, ram, tam, yam, Sam
ast	blast, cast, fast, last, mast, past, vast
ack	back, black, hack, jack, lack, sack
ar	bar, car, far, mar, scar, tar
at	bat, cat, fat, flat, pat, sat, that, vat
ate	bate, crate, date, rate, gate, grate, late, plate, rate, skate, state
aw	claw, draw, flaw, jaw, law, paw, raw, saw
eal	deal, meal, peal, real, seal, steal, veal
ean	bean, clean, dean, lean, mean
eat	beat, cleat, feat, meat, neat, seat, treat
ed	bed, bled, fled, led, pled, shed, sled, red, wed
eep	beep, cheep, creep, deep, jeep, keep, peep, sheep, sweep, weep
in	bin, chin, fin, pin, shin, tin, win
ing	bring, cling, fling, king, ring, sing, string, swing, thing
it	bit, fit, hit, kit, pit, skit, wit
ive	dive, drive, five, hive, live
ob	bob, cob, job, mob, rob, slob, sob
old	bold, cold, fold, gold, mold, sold, told
op	cop, chop, crop, drop, flop, hop, mop, pop, shop, stop, top
ope	cope, dope, hope, mope, pope, slope
ox	box, fox, lox, pox, sox
ump	bump, dump, grump, jump, lump, pump, slump, thump
un	bun, fun, gun, nun, pun, stun, sun
ust	bust, crust, dust, gust, just, must, rust, trust

FIGURE 3.5   Common Phonograms with Example Words.

Teaching Aids and References for Decoding by Analogy

Figure 3.5 provides a list of common phonograms. Teachers should keep in mind that this list is presented as a teaching reference, and is not intended to be reproduced for students to memorize or use without context.

Cunningham, P. (1995). *Phonics they use: Words for reading and writing.* New York: Harper Collins.

Fry, E., Kress, K., & Fountoukidis, D. (2000). *The reading teachers' book of lists.* West Nyack, NJ: The Center for Applied Research in Education.

Gaskins, I., Ehri, L., O'Hare, C., & Donnelly, K. (1997). Procedures for word learning: Making discoveries about words. *The Reading Teacher, 50,* 312–327.

Gaskins, R. W., J. C. Gaskins, et al. (1992). Using what you know to figure out what you don't know: An analogy approach to decoding. *Reading and Writing Quarterly—Overcoming Learning Difficulties, 8,* 197–221.

Wang, C. & Gaffney, J. (1998). First graders' use of analogy in word reading. *Journal of Literacy Research, 30,* 389–403.

SIGHT WORD DEVELOPMENT— SEMANTIC ORGANIZERS

A major goal of literacy instruction is for students to read with a high level of fluency so they can identify individual words and phrases used by an author with such rapidity that they can concentrate fully on the meaning of a text rather than using an inordinate amount of mental energy decoding words. We want decoding to become automatic and the act of reading always meaningful (Samuels, Schermer, & Reinking, 1992). The larger the number of words readers recognize instantly, the more rapidly text is decoded and, thus, the more fluent the readers.

As a reading specialist or classroom teacher, you are well aware of students who have a large number of words in their sight vocabulary and who read orally with great fluency, but who do not comprehend the text. These students have been identified as "word callers." They often are very successful readers in the early grades because the complexity of the text's meaning is minimal. Word callers are often referred to remedial reading classes because they "just don't understand a thing they read," although parents often herald these students as able to read "any book you hand them." It is important to help students and parents understand that reading is a meaning-making activity; without meaning, students are not reading.

A distinction between sight vocabularies and sight words should be made. All words have the potential to become part of an individual's sight vocabulary; mature avid readers have enormous sight vocabularies. Sight vocabularies also become specialized as readers enter into various fields of study. A word such as *pryazinamide* most likely is a sight word for physicians and pharmacists but not for the general public. By the way, pryazinamide is a drug used to treat tuberculosis.

Sight words are "a relatively small set of words in our language that do not conform to rules of pronunciation or analytical techniques learned by students beginning to read" (Gipe, 1995, p. 183). Included here are high-frequency words, which make up between 50% to 65% of all words in written text. The word lists compiled by Dolch (1935) and Fry et al. (1993) are examples of sight word lists that have been used by classroom teachers over the years as teaching references and study lists for students. These high-frequency, nonphonetic words are often the very words that cause some students to struggle with both reading and writing.

With this in mind, students do need to learn sight words and to continually add to their sight vocabularies throughout their years in school and beyond. Providing opportunities for students to read and reread books, poetry, and other text is perhaps the way for students to learn sight words. However, this may not be enough for some students.

Pehrsson and Robinson (1985) presented the semantic organizer approach to writing and reading instruction. This approach has many purposes for literacy instruction; one is improving sight vocabulary in a contextual setting. We have used this approach with many students at the Literacy Development Center.

Power of Semantic Organizers for Struggling Readers

- Students have multiple exposure to sight words within a known context.

- Students build their mental organizations or schema for words, which aids in recall.
- Students use sight words in reading and writing.
- Students learn indirectly how language functions in terms of parts of speech.

Steps to Follow

1. Collect a variety of pictures of objects, animals, and people that students can easily identify. Photographs from magazines as well as computer clip art work well. Paste the pictures on three 3 × 5 cards, print the picture names, and laminate.

2. Select three pictures of items that share an attribute that can be expressed in a single word and one picture of an item that doesn't have that attribute. For example, Figure 3.7a shows three different birds that fly and a dog that doesn't.

3. Show students the picture word cards and present other sight words that will allow them to create simple sentences orally.

4. Help students "read" the semantic organizer by clarifying that the single line means the presence of an attribute while the crossed line means the attribute is missing.

5. Either as a group or individually, have the students write the sentences generated by the semantic organizer.

Using Semantic Organizers with English Language Learners

As we have stated previously, it is extremely important that English language learners have opportunities for meaning-based literacy instruction. By their very nature, semantic organizers stress the relationship between words through attributes or characteristics. Begin the use of semantic organizers with ELL students by first presenting realia or picture clusters of two common objects such as a pen and a pencil and ask:

What are these objects?

How are they the same?

How are they different?

Now show three or four other pictures (chair, tree, crayon, apple)

What other objects could be put with the pencil and pen? Why?

This approach may seem very basic; the intent, however, is to provide ELL students with ways to make meaningful connections among known objects, begin to recognize the English word associated with them, and use oral language to describe the objects' characteristics or attributes.

Practice with other high-frequency words such as *run*, *walk*, and *jump*. Once ELL students can express the attributes of these motion words orally, follow the steps presented for the general use of semantic organizers.

Using Semantic Organizers to Improve Writing

In addition to realia and picture cluster semantic organizers, Pehrsson and Denner (1988) identified other semantic organizers that can help struggling writers develop sentences and paragraphs: verb, noun, concept, and episodic clusters. Verb and noun cluster organizers use pictures and words to represent action verbs and specific subjects, respectively. Students can generate sentences and short paragraphs as described in the Application and Example section.

Concept clusters and episodic clusters are more sophisticated. Concept clusters help students decide how related ideas can be organized. For example, through Figure 3.6a, students see how to organize their thoughts related to writing an autobiography. The organization for the autobiographies all start with the same five components but are personalized for each student when they add information unique to their own lives. Episodic clusters help students see relationships between events, cause and effect, and problem solutions. For example, in Figure 3.6b, as fourth graders begin their study of air pollution from a problem/solution organization, they used this episodic organizer to keep track of their learning and to prepare for writing a report.

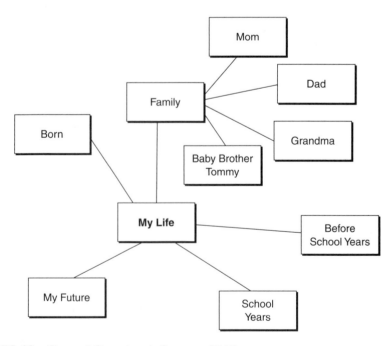

FIGURE 3.6A   Concept Organizer to Improve Writing.

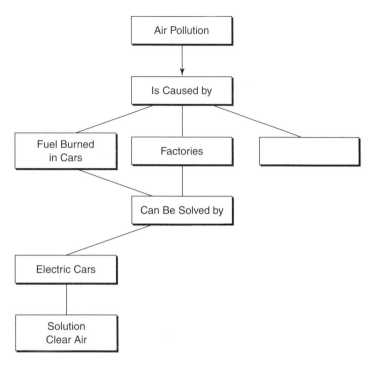

FIGURE 3.6B   Episodic Organizer: Problem/Solution.

Application and Example

Mrs. Elwood's second-grade class was studying living things. Several of the students were having difficulties with basic sight words. Mrs. Elwood brought those students together in a group to continue their understanding of living things and to reinforce sight word recognition. After sharing the picture words in Figure 3.7a (*owl, robin, parrot, dog*) and the functional sight words (*fly, bird, can, can't, is, isn't, it*), the students created the following text:

> An owl is a bird. It can fly. A robin is a bird.
> It can fly. A parrot is a bird. It can fly.
> A dog isn't a bird. It can't fly.

A few days later, Mrs. Elwood reviewed with students the paragraph they had written earlier and then introduced the semantic organizer shown in Figure 3.7b. She focused the students' attention on the change from *dog* to *penguin* and the sight word *but*.

After a science discussion on penguins, the students stated and then wrote the following:

> An owl is a bird. It can fly. A robin is a bird.
> It can fly. A parrot is a bird. It can fly.
> A penguin is a bird but it can't fly.

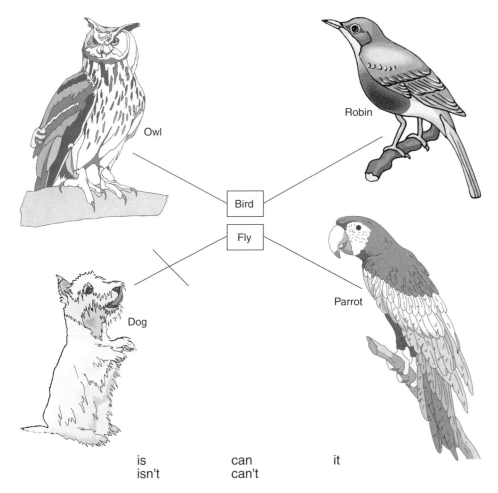

is   can   it
isn't   can't

FIGURE 3.7A   Semantic Organizer for Sight Word Development.

The students were encouraged to reread their paragraph for sight word reinforcement. Finally, the students were asked to think of how *and* could be used in their paragraph, which resulted in:

> An owl is a bird and it can fly. A robin is a bird and it can fly. A parrot is a bird and it can fly. A penguin is a bird but it can't fly.

Teaching Aids and References for Semantic Organizers

Sight word lists can be found on the Internet. For example, Fry's Instant Words can be found at:

http://www.sd129.org/hall/fry_words.html

and

www.usu.edu/teachall/text/reading/Frylist.pdf

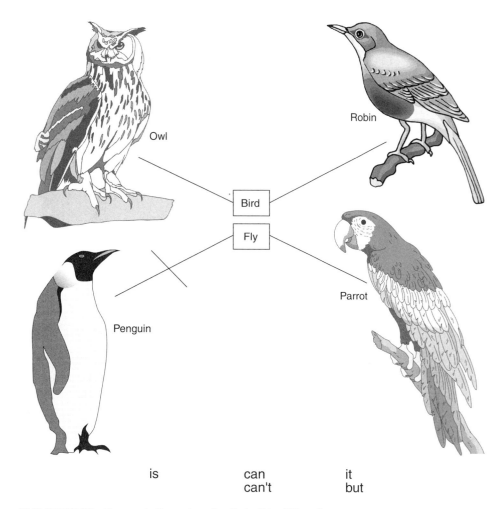

FIGURE 3.7B   Semantic Organizer for Sight Word Development.

Using sight words with a semantic organizer strategy helps students learn words in meaningful organizations rather than based solely on their frequency of use.

Dolch, E. (1935). *Dolch basic sight vocabulary*. Champaign, IL: Garrard.

Fry, E. B., Kress, J., & Fountoukidis, D. (1993). *The Reading Teachers' Book of Lists* 3/e. Englewood Cliffs, NJ: Prentice Hall.

Gipe, J. (1995) *Corrective reading techniques for the classroom teacher*. Scottsdale, AZ: Gorsuch Scarisbrick Publishers.

Pehrsson, R. S., & Denner, P. R. (1988). Semantic organizers: Implications for reading and writing. *Topics in Language Disorders Series, 8*(3), 24–37.

Pehrsson, R. S., & Robinson, H. A. (1985). *The semantic organizer approach to writing and reading instruction*. New York: Aspen Publishers.

Samuels, S., Schermer, N., & Reinking, D. (1992). Reading fluency: Techniques for making decoding automatic. In S. Samuels & A. Farstrup (Eds.), *What research has to say about reading instruction* (pp. 124–144). Newark, DE: International Reading Association.

SIGHT WORD DEVELOPMENT—CLOZE ACTIVITIES

The high-frequency, nonphonetic words that often cause readers great difficulty can become more friendly if students understand that these words are a natural part of our oral language and that many of these words are very predictable if the readers read with meaning in mind. Taylor (1953) presented the cloze procedure as a method for determining text readability. His work is based on the psychological phenomena that the human mind always wants to have things completed, resulting in a sense of closure. For example, if you saw the following, your mind would want to complete the drawing and form a triangle.

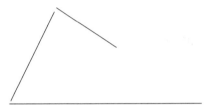

In relationship to reading and language, our mind works the same way and wants to complete the sentence or phrase read or uttered. Think about how often it has happened that you are able to complete your friend's or mate's sentence before he or she does. We are able to do this because we share the same context and because our language is both redundant and predictable.

Goodman's work also provides insight into the connection between language and reading (1968). He defined reading as a "psycholinguistic guessing game." Goodman suggested that because of our understanding of oral language, we can easily predict or guess what the next word will be in oral and written text. While all literacy educators and researchers may not agree with this definition, it does assist teachers as they work with struggling readers. For example, in the sentence, "I like to eat_____ ," there are many possible answers but not an infinite number because language pattern words already used start to limit the possible guesses. Responses from students such as *bananas* or *peaches* indicate that for the student (a) language is meaning based and (b) comprehension is occurring.

The number of responses is further limited when students focus on the graphophonemes present in the word when the missing word is provided: "I like to eat *popcorn*." Now, given the responses *bananas* and *peaches*, *peaches* is the better choice. The guess is still incorrect, however. If the sentence is in isolation, then readers must rely on their decoding knowledge because they do not know it by sight. If, as is usually the case for authentic written text, more context is provided either before or after the unknown word, readers can more accurately predict the correct response. "I like to eat *popcorn*. I enjoy it at the movies." Because of a shared language and social experiences, the missing word has to be *popcorn*.

The cloze procedure utilizes this knowledge of language and society. Taylor's procedure originally focused on using cloze as a way to determine the readability of a text in terms of how well a reader and author are matched. The cloze procedure is also a valuable tool through which struggling readers can learn sight words and develop their sight vocabularies.

A note of caution is included here. Some struggling readers may find cloze activities frustrating especially when given "worksheets" to complete independently and when they are required to provide one specific word. We highly recommend that teachers use cloze activities as interactive teaching lessons so that students receive immediate feedback and support. Also, we have listed two computer programs that use cloze activities. Students may find these products motivating but they may also be just as frustrating to some as paper-and-pencil activities.

The Power of Cloze Activities for Struggling Readers

- Students use their knowledge of oral language to help them read unknown written words. It is especially helpful for second language learners.

- Students continue to reinforce their understanding that reading is a meaning-making activity.

- Students build their self-confidence and are willing to take risks to predict unknown words.

Steps to Follow

1. Build from oral language. Depending on the oral language abilities of the students, the teacher may begin with picture word cards. For example, show students related pairs of words such as *boy/girl*, *dog/cat*, *in/out*, and *up/down*. Have them listen to sentences and supply the missing words:

   The dog ran up the stairs so the cat ran _____ the stairs. The boy chased the girl in and _____ of the door.

2. Do the same exercises with written text. Discuss how the structure of the sentence helps to make the prediction of the missing word more accurate.

3. Expand the amount of text and have the students read along as you read and think aloud to model the thought process. The text in Figure 3.8 is taken from *I Like to Be Little* by Charlotte Zolotow (Harper & Row, 1987).

4. First read the passage completely, saying *blank* for the missing words. Tell the students that the author leaves clues in the sentences so that you can predict missing words correctly. Then begin to model your thought process. For example: "There is a blank in the first sentence but, the author helps me by using the word *her* in the second sentence. I also know that two people are talking to each other because I see

Once there was a little _____ .
"What do you want to be when you grow _____ ?" her mother asked.
"I just want to stay _____ right now," she said.
"Why?" said her _____ . "It's nice to be grown _____ . Why do you want to be little?"
"Because I am," said the little girl, "and _____ when you are little you can do things you _____ do when you grow up."

FIGURE 3.8   Cloze Text to Improve Sight Word Development.

quotation marks. One person is the mother. The missing word in the first sentence most likely is *girl*."

5. Continue in like manner, gradually having the students take over the think aloud.

6. Have students work with a partner on a similar passage that reinforces some of the same sight words. Provide them with several opportunities to practice the strategy.

7. Provide excerpts from other students' books in which the author provides the reader with enough support to make predictions. Have the students write their predictions in the blank, then check the original text for accuracy.

Using Cloze Activities with English Language Learners

Because cloze activities are meaning based, cloze activities for ELL students can be found in books and websites for students of all ages. For example, the University of Victoria has an online English Language Study Center (http://web2.uvcs.uvic.ca/elc/studyzone/index.htm) through which mature students can improve their understanding of written English through short story and cloze passage self-assessment.

Fables are good text sources when first introducing cloze to ELL students. Since they convey universal truths, students from any culture can relate to their meaning. For example, through the story of the ant and the grasshopper, you can increase sight word recognition by first telling ELL students:

> Listen as I read the story of *The Ant and the Grasshopper* (Poole, 2000) for the words that tell about the two insects.

After reading the story, ask students to provide "ant" words and "grasshopper" words while you write them for class display. Finally, provide a copy of the story with deleted words for the students to complete with a partner.

Using Cloze Activities to Improve Writing

Cloze activities can improve students' writing by helping them think about semantic alternatives to convey their thoughts. Use examples of student writing and focus on verbs, adjectives, and adverbs. For example, this second grader's story is basic but has clear ideas:

> My dog's name is Winston. He is a cocker spaniel.
> He can jump for a treat. He gets me up in the
> morning for his food.

Present the story as is on an overhead. Then prepare the story on an overhead as follows:

> My dog's name is Winston. He is a _____ spaniel. He
> can _____ for a treat. He _____ me up
> in the morning to get his food.

Through oral discussion, ask students to suggest words that help the reader know more about Winston.

Application and Example

A variation on cloze is maze or multiple choice cloze. Maze may be easier for some students because choices are presented to help the readers. For each missing word, three word choices are provided in random order: a word from the same part of speech, the correct response, and a word that isn't meaningful in the text.

Joy, a tutor at the Literacy Development Center, decided to use the maze strategy prior to using cloze with Alicia, a second grader who was having difficulty with sight words. Joy first read *I Like to Be Little* (Zolotow, 1987) in its entirety to Alicia as she followed along. After discussing the story, Joy showed Alicia the text in Figure 3.9 written on a lapboard. Using a think-aloud procedure similar to the one for cloze, Joy helped Alicia decide which words were the best choices.

Joy prepared a second passage for Alicia to write on as she considered the choices for the missing word. To keep Alicia thinking about the

Once there was a little _____ (boy, girl, out).

"What do you want to be when you grow

_____ ?" (fire, down, up) her mother asked.

"I just want to stay _____ (little, big, water)

right now," she said.

FIGURE 3.9   A Maze Passage.

importance of making meaning when reading, she would ask questions such as:

"Why did you pick that word?"

"Does that word make sense for you?"

"What clues in the sentence did you use to help you?"

Once Alicia had completed the exercise, Joy gave her the book so Alicia could check her own responses with the real text.

Teaching Aids and References for Cloze Activities

Aesop Fables
http://www.aesopfables.com

ClozePro by CRICK SOFTWARE
http://www.cricksoft.com

Diascriptive® Cloze & Writing Practice Activities by GAMCO
http://www.gamco.com/products.htm

Goodman, K. (1968). The psycholinguistic nature of the reading process. In K. S. Goodman (Ed.), *The psycholinguistic nature of the reading process.* Detroit: Wayne State Press.

Taylor, W. (1953). Cloze procedure: A new tool for measuring readability. *Journalism Quarterly, 30,* 415–433.

Children's Reading References

Poole, A. L. (2000). *The ant and the grasshopper.* New York: Holiday House.

Zolotow, C. (1987). *I like to be little.* New York: Harper & Row.

VOCABULARY DEVELOPMENT—MULTIPLE-MEANING

How many definitions can you think of for the word *run*? Let's see:

Moving very fast

A run in my stockings

A dog runs

Running for the presidency

The refrigerator is running

All of these definitions are possible as well as many more. If you look in the dictionary, you will find more than 125 definitions and contextual meaning uses for the word *run* (Webster, 1998).

Good readers know that the appropriate definition for the word *run* depends on the context in which it is used. Struggling readers may be very able to decode the word and know its meaning in one context, but cannot comprehend a text that uses a different meaning for the word. Meyerson, Ford, Jones & Ward (1991) showed how third and fifth graders can easily apply the wrong definition to known words even when given the context for the definition. Thus, building sight vocabulary also implies an understanding of which meaning fits the given context.

Teachers are often puzzled by young readers who decode multiple-meaning words correctly but who fail to comprehend what they've read. Wide reading in many different types of text will aid many struggling readers to learn new meanings for known words; for others, more direct instruction may be needed. Teachers should also keep in mind that there is a developmental aspect to learning new meanings for known words as documented in *The Living Vocabulary* (Dale & O'Rourke, 1979).

The Power of Multiple-Meaning Words for Struggling Readers

- Students already recognize the word, so decoding isn't a problem.
- Most of the common multiple-meaning words are words in students' oral language if their first language is English. Multiple-meaning words often cause confusion for second language learners and require many exposures in meaningful text.
- Students' awareness that reading and writing are meaning-making thought processes is heightened.

Steps to Follow

1. Select three to five words to be taught in one lesson.
2. Present the words on the board or overhead. Give the students the same words on cards (see Figure 3.10 for examples).

about	run	spell	can
will	down	mean	right
page	letter	saw	band
state	hard	above	have
back	set	well	on
head	bank	high	face
by	use	book	last
miss	side	light	off
point	left	take	cut
over	home	get	

FIGURE 3.10   Some Common High-Frequency Multiple-Meaning Words.

3. Use one of the words in a written sentence and ask the students to provide a meaning for the word. For example:

    (a) My mother asked me to *set* the table before dinner.

4. After the students have agreed on a definition, present a new sentence.

    (b) Jamie was always 10 minutes late for school, so his mother _____ the clock ahead 10 minutes.

5. Ask the students to hold up the word that best fits the sentence from the cards they have.

6. Discuss how *set* is the correct answer in sentence B as well as A. What definition can you give for *set* in sentence B? How is the meaning different for the word *set* in the two sentences?

7. Ask the students if they can think of another definition for *set* or how they have heard people use the word in a different way. They may suggest *set*, as in "set the book on the table," or *set*, as in "ready, set, go."

8. Repeat the steps for the other words in the lesson.

Using Multiple-Meaning Words with English Language Learners

English is a difficult language to learn; multiple-meaning words make it confusing. Students will be able to learn the different definitions of a multiple-meaning word when they hear and read it in a meaningful context.

Research suggests that students in third and fifth grade assign the wrong meaning to words even when told the general category of a word such as *organ* as a science word and not a musical instrument (Meyerson, Ford, Jones, & Ward, 1991). It is, thus, very important that we present content-specific vocabulary words that also have multiple meanings in a way that all students, especially second language learners, comprehend the associated meaning. This includes the use of photographs, videos, and appropriate websites as well as accompanying text from text and trade books.

Using Multiple-Meaning Words to Improve Writing

As a writer I seldom think about which meaning of a word I need for a sentence since I know the context in which it is used supports the correct meaning. For example:

That was a very light book; it didn't cause me to think very much.

The meaning I want to convey is that the book was easy to read. Immature readers may think the book doesn't weigh very much or that it was light in color. Readers who understand the function of the semicolon know that the book was very easy reading for me.

At the same time, I must be sure my readers understand my meaning and so I try to use the most appropriate words to convey my message. You can help young writers become aware of the effects of their writing through conferencing and questioning when their meaning is ambiguous.

What meaning did you want in this sentence?

How can you help the reader understand that meaning?

What word could you add or remove?

Application and Example

Dottie's second graders who attended the reading improvement program were having fun listening to Dottie read *Amelia Bedelia* books. After sharing several with them, Dottie selected the word *light* for the second graders to explore for multiple meanings:

Turn off the *light*

Light the candle

The baby doesn't weigh much; she is *light* as a feather

Light toast, not dark

The dawn's early *light*

A *light* touch

Dottie then asked the students to illustrate a correct meaning of light along with a way Amelia Bedelia might interpret it. Rico's picture appears in Figure 3.11.

Teaching Aids and References for Multiple-Meaning Words

Dale, E., & O'Rourke, J. (1979). *The living vocabulary.* Palo Alto, CA: Field Educational Publications.

Meyerson, M. J., Ford, M. S., Jones, W. P., & Ward, M. A. (1991). Science vocabulary knowledge of third and fifth grade students. *Science Education*, 74(4), 419–428.

Random House Webster's Unabridged Dictionary. (1988).

FIGURE 3.11   Illustration of Multiple Meanings for the Word *Light*.

WORKING WITH MIDDLE SCHOOL STUDENTS TO IMPROVE WORD RECOGNITION: WORD FORMS

Middle school students often are challenged by the vocabulary in the content areas of science and social studies. These words should become part of their ever-growing sight vocabulary. In order to do this, middle school students benefit from instruction that helps them understand the meaning and spelling relationships between word forms. Bear, Invernizzi, Templeton, and Johnson (2004) include the notion of word form at the derivational relation stage of word study.

The Power of Word Forms for Middle School Students

- Middle school students focus on understanding the relationships between vocabulary and spelling.
- Students use the dictionary or thesaurus with a concentrated purpose.
- Students develop confidence to read challenging text.

Steps to Follow

1. After the students read a section from a textbook or article from the newspaper, select three or four words that have different forms. For example, in a newspaper article on the development of the Internet, *authenticate* was used. Discuss the meaning of the word.

2. Write the focus word on the board or overhead next to its appropriate question word (part of speech):

   Who? (noun)
   What? (verb)   *authenticate*
   How? (adjective/adverb)

3. Tell the students to reread the sentence containing the focus word and then ask: *What word does* authenticate *remind you of if you were thinking about a person? What is the noun form of* authenticate?

4. Encourage students to refer to the dictionary or thesaurus for assistance.

5. Compare the spelling between the two words.

   Who? (noun)   *author*
   What? (verb)   *authenticate*
   How? (adjective/adverb)

6. Ask students to find other forms of the word such as adjective or adverb:

   Who? (noun)   *author*
   What? (verb)   *authenticate*
   How? (adjective)   *authentic*

7. Challenge the students to create a sentence in which all forms are used:

   The *author* of a book on painting was able to *authenticate* that the watercolor was *authentic*.

Teaching Aids and References for Word Forms

Figure 3.12 contains a list of word forms helpful for instruction. Post these and other word forms in the classroom to develop a middle school word wall.

Bear, D., Invernizzi, M., Templeton, S., & Johnson, F. (2004). *Words their way: Word study for phonics, vocabulary and spelling instruction.* Upper Saddle River, NJ: Merrill Prentice Hall.

actor	native	reactionary
action	nationalize	react
actually	national	reactive
author	informer	prognosticator
authenticate	information	prognosticate
authentic	informative	prognostic
critic	professional	confidant
criticize	profess	confidence
critical	professionally	confidently

FIGURE 3.12   Word Forms.

ASSESSING WORD RECOGNITION

Why assess word recognition? Fluent readers spend less time decoding because they recognize words automatically; this allows them to concentrate on meaning. The automatic identification of words and the understanding of their relationship in text is the foundation of comprehension. Through an assessment of students' recognition of commonly used words, you can gain insight into fluency development as well as where to focus instructional efforts.

Sight Word Recognition

Our experiences with sight word assessments have included the use of a variety of published lists such as the Dolch List, Fry's Instant Words, word lists from basal series, and the placement list found in many informal reading inventories. A word is considered to be part of students' sight vocabulary when it is recognized within 5 seconds without analyzing the word.

When preparing to give a sight word assessment, we suggest that you present 8 to 10 words at a time to individual students and ask them to read the list orally as quickly as possible. Have one list for the students and a duplicate list to keep track of the words orally pronounced correctly by the student.

The lists are usually organized from "easier" to "harder" words. This difficulty level is sometimes misleading because some students may have difficulty with a word such as *when* on Fry's first 100 words and be able to read *school* on the third 100 list.

Assessing Decoding Skills

When skilled readers encounter a word they do not know by sight, they apply a variety of strategies to decode the word. Some of the strategies they use include analogies, syllabication, and using context clues. Only

First Hundred

the	or	will	number	he	we	some	call	at	she
of	one	no	had	was	when	her	who	two	get
up	and	other	by	for	your	would	oil	be	do
about	way	could	to	on	can	make	its	more	come
a	word	out	people	are	said	like	now	this	how
in	but	many	my	as	there	him	find	write	made
is	not	then	than	with	use	into	long	have	their
you	what	them	first	his	an	time	down	go	may
that	all	these	water	they	each	has	day	from	if
it	were	so	been	I	which	look	dig	see	part

Second Hundred

over	say	set	try	live	mean	such	away	name	also
new	great	put	kind	me	old	because	animal	land	still
sound	where	end	hand	back	any	turn	house	good	around
take	help	does	picture	give	same	here	point	different	learn
only	through	another	again	most	tell	why	page	sentence	form
little	much	well	change	very	boy	ask	letter	home	should
work	before	large	off	after	follow	went	mother	man	three
know	line	must	play	thing	came	men	answer	us	America
place	right	big	spell	our	want	read	found	think	small
year	too	even	air	just	show	need	study	move	world

Third Hundred

high	saw	important	miss	last	next	sea	let	light	together
every	left	until	idea	school	hard	began	above	hear	song
near	don't	children	enough	father	open	grow	girl	thought	got
add	few	side	cat	keep	example	took	sometimes	stop	being
food	while	feet	face	tree	begin	river	mountain	head	group
between	along	car	watch	never	filed	four	cut	without	leave
own	might	mile	far	start	always	carry	young	under	often
below	close	night	Indian	city	those	state	talk	second	family
country	something	walk	really	earth	both	once	soon	story	run
plant	seem	white	almost	eye	paper	book	list	later	it's

Common suffixes: -s, -ing, -ed, -er, -ly, -est

FIGURE 3.13   Fry's First 300 Instant Words. (From: *Reading Teachers' Book of Lists*, 3rd edition by Edward Fry, Jacqueline Kress, & Dona Lee Fountoukidis. Copyright © 2003. This material is used by permission of John Wiley & Sons, Inc.)

when all else fails do skilled readers apply their sound/symbol association knowledge and try to decode a word phonetically.

When we work with struggling readers at the Literacy Development Center, we try to determine what strategies students have for determining unknown words. One easy method is to use the results from sight word assessment. Let's say you are using Fry's Instant Words (Figure 3.13). On the second 100 list, a fourth grader did not recognize these words instantly:

found

before

different

picture

after

Present these words to the student on individual 3 × 5 cards. "These are words that you had some difficulties with when I asked you to read the lists earlier. If you take your time, can you tell me what they are? Try this first one." If the student does not know how to proceed, suggest: "What sound do you hear in the beginning of the word? What sound do you hear at the end? In the middle?" In this way, you will gain an understanding of the student's knowledge of initial and final consonants and vowels. With a word such as *different*, insight into how a student handles a multisyllabic word can also be gained. Other unknown sight words can be placed into sentences to see if a student uses context clues.

PART IV

When Struggling Readers and Writers Need to Improve Fluency

Rasinski (1989) provided a general definition of fluency: the smooth and natural oral production of written text. May (1998) defined fluency as not mere speed, but the ability to follow the writer's message while reading in natural-sounding phrases. He described fluent readers' interactions with text as constantly making predictions about the words that are coming up next. Their eyes jump ahead to confirm their predictions, while their short-term memories hold the word being spoken.

When struggling readers are experiencing problems with fluency, their oral reading is hesitant, halting, and choppy. Comprehension is affected as the writer's intent is lost in the reader's lack of flow from one thought to the next. Ignoring punctuation, the words on the page are not read in meaningful phrases. Sometimes words are read one-by-one with no logical links made between them. Other times, substituted words disrupt or change the meaning of the passage. Insertions, omissions, and mispronunciations also inhibit fluency.

Nonfluent readers exhibit very little expression in their oral reading; their intonation does not reflect the meaning of the text. The automaticity theory (LaBerge & Samuels, 1974) proposed that nonfluent readers' comprehension is affected by the amount of time and attention that they spend decoding words. Fluent readers, however, spend less time decoding because they recognize words automatically; this allows them to concentrate on meaning. Reutzel and Cooter (1999) described the fluent reader as one who reads accurately, naturally, and with relative ease. Rasinski (1989) noted that repetition, as the key to fluency, necessitates practice with a text until a criterion level is met. Although repetition may seem to be tedious and uninviting, Rasinski noted ways to use typical classroom events to integrate repeated readings of text.

The strategies described in this section can all be integrated with the day-to-day literacy routines and practices in the classroom. Many of the strategies that promote fluency also have a positive effect on motivation. Students build confidence as they track their progress or hear themselves, individually or as part of a group, reading with expression and intonation. The following strategies address the issues that impact reading fluency. The strategies empower struggling readers with tools to improve their fluency and, in turn, their ability to communicate and to understand the written word.

REPEATED READING

Repeated reading was first suggested as a strategy to improve fluency by Samuels (1979). This method evolved from his earlier automaticity theory (LaBerge & Samuels, 1974), which stated that fluent readers decode text automatically. The procedure includes the rereading of a meaningful passage until a satisfactory level of fluency, determined by the reading rate and number of errors, is reached. Students practice their passages (50 to 200 words) in an assisted, unassisted, or paired repeated reading model and return to the teacher when they are ready to have their next rereading timed and documented (Dowhower, 1989; Koskinen & Blum, 1986).

Samuels (1979) noted that keeping a record of the repeated readings in graph form is very motivating for the students; tape recordings of the readings may also be used to demonstrate growth in fluency. Teachers can involve parents in the process by occasionally sending a practice passage home, along with an explanation of the benefits of repeated readings. Students enjoy watching their own progress, as their reading rate increases, by graphing timed repeated reading results.

Several authors have provided charts of recommended reading rates by grade level (Flynt & Cooter, 2004: Harris & Sipay, 1990; Rasinski & Padak, 2000). The following range of words-per-minute rates are found:

(a) first grade: 60–90;

(b) second grade: 70–120;

(c) third grade: 80–140;

(d) fourth grade: 90–170; and

(e) fifth grade: 100–195.

Given these wide ranges, we recommend goals be set in reasonable increments for each student's individual needs.

The Power of Repeated Reading for Struggling Readers

As struggling readers practice their passages using the repeated reading strategy, they progress from word-by-word decoding to reading with more ease and expression. This builds their confidence and increases their comprehension as they are better able to concentrate on the meaning of the passage. The benefits are abundant; repeated reading of a passage provides the following for the struggling reader (Dowhower, 1989; Samuels, 1997):

- Increased reading rate
- The transfer of increased reading rate to new text
- Increased comprehension
- The transfer of increased comprehension to new text (at the same reading level)
- Increased phraseology and expression

Steps to Follow

1. Select a meaningful passage (50 to 200 words).
2. Time the student as the passage is read aloud. Keep track of the errors, and record the data on a graph. Help the student to set a realistic fluency goal over the next few weeks. See Form 4 in the Appendix.
3. Direct the student to practice reading the passage alone, with assistance, or with a partner.
4. Repeat Step 2 when the student is once again ready for a timed reading to record on the graph.
5. Direct the student to continue practicing and recording until the fluency goal is met.
6. Once the goal is met, select a new passage and begin the procedure again.

Using Repeated Reading with English Language Learners

Repeated reading of texts is equally important for learners of English. Rasinski (2000) recommended implementing repeated reading in authentic activities in the classroom. He suggested integrating performances of poetry and Readers' Theater into the instructional activities of the classroom. Suggestions for use of poetry can be found in this section under the choral reading strategy. Also in this section, we have provided step-by-step procedures for employing Readers' Theater.

To extend repeated reading beyond the school day, Koskinen, Blum, Bisson, Phillips, Creamer, and Baker (1999) suggested providing books with accompanying audiotapes for ELL students to take home and practice rereading. This is especially important for students who speak only their native language at home and who have few, if any, English texts in their homes.

After providing many opportunities for ELL students to practice repeated readings through poetry, Readers' Theater, or individual or paired readings in the classroom, invite them to participate in the timed readings. They, too, can then begin to chart their reading rates on graphs.

Using Repeated Reading to Improve Writing

According to the Northwest Regional Educational Laboratory (2001), fluency is one writing trait that should be developed and assessed. Sentence fluency is "the rhythm and flow of the language, the sound of word patterns, the way in which the writing plays to the ear, not just to the eye. Fluent writing has cadence, power, rhythm, and movement. It is free of awkward word patterns that slow readers' progress" (www.nwrel.org/assessment).

By exposing students to good writing found in children's literature as well as examples from students themselves, they may begin to see and hear the connection between the flow of oral and written language. For example, young children and second language learners often do not realize that the phrase "once upon a time" is made of four separate words and are surprised when they see the phrase in print. Likewise, when they try to write a fairy tale, they may write the phrase as a giant word, *onceuponatime*. While it can be argued that young children who do this have not fully developed their concept of word, this is also an example of how fluent readers chunk common phrases when reading orally so that they are heard as one word.

Students can improve their writing skills along with their reading fluency when teachers encourage them to read and reread their own writing aloud as they go through the writing process. They can read it to a peer or just to themselves in a quiet voice. This will develop their ear for language; it is sometimes easier to fix an awkward sentence or phrase when we hear it rather than rereading it silently.

Application and Examples

The repeated reading strategy is incorporated easily into a variety of classroom structures. Dottie has recommended several different formats for her student teachers to utilize in the Language Arts Block:

(a) Unassisted model—practicing alone, the student uses a stopwatch or timer for independent monitoring of the reading rate (Dowhower, 1989).

(b) Assisted model—a knowledgeable other (a classroom aide or parent volunteer) can provide the appropriate model, or a tape recording of the passage can be used in a listening center (Dowhower, 1989).

(c) Paired Repeated Reading—students work with partners, but practice their own selected passage (Koskinen & Blum, 1986). First, the students practice silently, and then each reads the passage aloud three times to the partner. Following the readings, the students self-assess their performance and receive positive feedback about their improved reading rate from the partner.

One of the Paradise School student teachers reported to Dottie on the success of her implementation of repeated readings in a second-grade classroom. Joseph and Edward were partners in the Paired Repeated Reading model. Joseph was a struggling reader, working hard to move beyond a beginning first-grade reading level. The student teacher worked with him on several strategies to improve his fluency. Every day he asked to practice with his partner. The book he was rereading for the timings was *My Friend Edward Cole* (Bradman, 1996). The student teacher explained that Joseph chose the book with a main character named Edward partly because that was also the name of his repeated reading buddy. In the book, the character Edward Cole is a boy who tells a different exaggerated story about himself on each new page. The repeated line at the end of every page except the last is, "But I don't believe him." The two students worked diligently together, keeping graphs of their timed readings. Joseph's goal was to reach 85 words per minute.

One day, following their session, the boys approached the student teacher, giggling together and eager to talk to her. Joseph proudly reported that he had reached his 85 words-per-minute goal. He added that his buddy Edward had shown him the latest timing on the graph. Joseph could now say the last line in the book about not only the character Edward Cole but his buddy, Edward, "I believe him, I believe him!"

Teaching Aids and References for Repeated Reading

For a reproducible graph for charting repeated readings, see the Appendix, Form 4.

Professional References

Dowhower, S. L. (1989). Repeated reading: Research into practice. *The Reading Teacher*, *42*, 502–507.

Flynt, E. S., & Cooter, R. B., Jr. (2004). *Reading inventory of the classroom* (5th ed.). Upper Saddle River, NJ: Pearson.

Harris, A. J., & Sipay, E. R. (1990). *How to increase reading ability* (8th ed.). New York: Longman.

Koskinen, P. S., & Blum, I. H. (1986). Paired repeated reading: A classroom strategy for developing fluent reading. *The Reading Teacher*, *40*, 70–75.

Koskinen, P. S., Blum, I. H., Bisson, S. A., Phillips, S. M., Creamer, T. S., & Baker, T. K. (1999). Shared reading, books, and audiotapes: Supporting diverse students in school and at home. *The Reading Teacher*, *52*(5), 430–444.

LaBerge, D., & Samuels, S. J. (1974). Toward a theory of automatic information processing in reading. *Cognitive Psychology*, *6*, 294–323.

May, F. B. (1998). *Reading as communication*. Upper Saddle River, NJ: Merrill/Prentice Hall.

Northwest Regional Educational Laboratory. (2001). The real thing: Six traits of NWREL's writing model. Retrieved August 12, 2004, from http://www.nwrel.org/assessment.

Rasinski, T. V. (1989). Fluency for everyone: Incorporating fluency instruction in the classroom. *The Reading Teacher*, *42*, 690–693.

Rasinski, T. V. (2000). Speed does matter in reading. *The Reading Teacher*, *53*(2) 146–150.

Rasinski, T. V., & Padak, N. (2000). *Effective reading strategies: Teaching children who find reading difficult* (2nd ed.). Upper Saddle River, NJ: Merrill.

Reutzel, D. R., & Cooter, R. B., Jr. (1999). *Balanced reading strategies and practices: Assessing and assisting readers with special needs.* Upper Saddle River, NJ: Merrill/Prentice Hall.

Samuels, S. J. (1979). The method of repeated readings. *The Reading Teacher, 32,* 403–408.

Samuels, S. J. (1997). The method of repeated readings. *The Reading Teacher, 50*(5), 376–381 (reprint).

Children's Book References

Bradman, T. (1996). *My friend Edward Cole.* Boston, MA: Houghton Mifflin.

READERS' THEATER

Readers' Theater is a performance of text. It focuses on the oral interpretation of the words in a script (Sloyer, 1982). Students use literature, poems, songs, or scenarios that they write themselves. The essence of the performance of the script is in the oral reading, not in the use of props, costumes, or actions.

Presentations can be modified in a variety of ways. In some classrooms, students sit in a row of chairs or stools that are set up in front of their audience. Sometimes the students stand in front of the class. One interesting way of presenting the performance resembles a revolving door. All of the readers stand shoulder to shoulder in front of their audience, but with their backs turned. As students take turns reading their parts, they pivot around to face the audience, say their lines, and turn back again. As one back is being turned toward the audience, a different reader is turning to face the audience.

The Power of Readers' Theater for Struggling Readers

Participating in a Readers' Theater presentation helps build struggling readers' fluency, comprehension, and confidence. Knowing their own limitations in oral reading, nonfluent readers are hesitant to participate in reading activities in front of an audience. By being a member of a Readers' Theater group, struggling readers have the opportunity to feel confident reading in front of an audience. Walker (1996) indicated three different learner patterns that produce increased engagement with Readers' Theater:

- Students who communicate through drama will find this to be a natural way to develop fluency.
- Word-bound decoders, who do not identify with characters, will naturally make connections with characters through the scripts.

■ For students who have difficulty tracking, a short Readers' Theater script provides a purposeful reason to track.

Steps to Follow

1. Decide on a script to use for the Readers' Theater presentation. It can come from literature the students are reading; a song, a poem, or a familiar folk tale; or the students can write the script themselves.
2. Assign lines or let the students work out the parts among themselves.
3. Direct the students to practice, concentrating on expression, intonation, and dramatic effect.
4. Provide a venue and audience for the students' performance when they are ready.

Using Readers' Theater with English Language Learners

Hadaway, Vardell, and Young (2002) discussed Readers' Theater as a benefit for oral language development of ELL students because it includes purposeful oral reading, cooperative learning, an opportunity to use oral skills, and increased attentiveness in listening. In addition, they noted it is an important technique for enhancing reading ability. Diaz-Rico (2004) concurred the benefits of Readers' Theater extend beyond the improvement of fluency. She suggested criteria for teachers' evaluations of performances: (a) smooth delivery of lines, (b) clear and distinct speech, (c) fluent reading, (d) creation of believable characters, (e) listening and reacting to other characters appropriately, and (f) mature onstage behaviour. She added, ". . . Readers' Theater makes a substantial contribution to students' growth in reading skills, communicative competence, and social awareness and interpersonal cooperation in the English development classroom" (p. 218).

Using Readers' Theater to Improve Writing

When students first begin performing Readers' Theaters, they may use previously prepared scripts. However, the next step is for them to write their own scripts. Beginning readers will be working with repetitive, predictable texts that may already include much dialogue. This could be a starting point for their scripts as they transfer some of the dialogue from text and then add their own creative adaptations to the story. Peregoy and Boyle (2005) explained when English learners reach the intermediate level, they are ready to move on from reading, interpreting, and performing scripts to developing and writing them as well. This next level of interaction with text requires students to identify the most important events and characters in a story. Then they must analyze their own interpretations of characters, plots, and resolutions to produce appropriate dialogue for the script and subsequent performance.

Middle school students can work together to develop not only the dialogue of the characters but also that of the narrator (Cecil & Gipe, 2003). Each student may take on the part of more than one character. The performers develop dialogue that they can read fluently and use tone of voice and facial expression to allow the audience to visualize their thoughts. Writing Readers' Theater scripts enriches the meaning of texts and makes the reading/writing connection for struggling, ELL, and middle school students.

Application and Examples

Scripts for Readers' Theaters are available from a number of resources. The school librarian often has copies of scripts of familiar folk tales. Books of plays for students from the public library can be adapted for Readers' Theaters; and commercially prepared scripts are available at teacher resource centers. To personalize the experience for students, scripts may be created from a text that has been read by the participating students.

After reading *The Worst Team Ever* (Kessler, 1985), Dottie and a student she was tutoring wrote the following script, chose characters, and rehearsed their performance. Most of the dialogue came directly from the pages of the story, which lent itself well to this activity. The student enjoyed the practice, which helped increase fluency and build confidence. He always looked forward to the last line of the dialogue, borrowed from a movie character; and no matter how many times he practiced, he couldn't help but laugh when he got to that part. The Readers' Theater was performed by the tutor and her student as the culminating activity of the parent conference.

The Worst Team Ever
Written and Illustrated by Leonard Kessler
Adapted for Readers' Theater
by Dottie Kulesza

Melvin Moose:	Look at this.
Bobo Bullfrog:	It says that our team is the worst swamp ball team ever. We lost 35 games in a row.
Melvin Moose:	Maybe you need a new coach.
Bobo Bullfrog:	We don't have a coach. The last one quit.
Melvin Moose:	That is a job for Old Turtle.
Bobo Bullfrog:	He once won the coach of the year prize. Here comes Old Turtle now. Ask him. Ask him.
Melvin Moose:	Hi, Old Turtle. The Green Hoppers need a new coach.
Bobo Bullfrog:	Do you want the job?
Old Turtle:	The Green Hoppers? They lost 35 games in a row.
Bobo Bullfrog:	We need a good coach.

Melvin Moose:	They need you, Old Turtle. There is only one more game.
Bobo Bullfrog:	We want to win that last game.
Old Turtle:	I will coach the Green Hoppers if Melvin will help me.
Bobo Bullfrog:	Can you be our coach next year, too?
Old Turtle:	Let's see how we do in the last game.
Bobo Bullfrog:	Good job, Old Turtle, we won the game!
Old Turtle:	The players worked hard. They did a good job.
Bobo Bullfrog:	We hope you can coach us next year.
Old Turtle:	I'll be back!!

Readers' Theater scripts can also be designed to include choral reading lines. Dottie's remedial reading students always enjoy this activity. It motivates them to read, increases their fluency, and builds their confidence. This is a powerful strategy, especially for third and fourth grade students who are reading at a first or second grade level, because it helps them feel successful reading in front of their peers. One of the students' favorites is directly from *Can You Carry It, Harriet?* (Buston, 1989). Dottie typed out the text, using a repetitive verse as the choral reading lines. After they practiced, the students asked their classroom teacher if they could perform for their class:

All:	(Title) Can you carry it, Harriet?
Student 1:	Here is a bee, all yellow and black, with four little wings upon its back.
All:	Can you carry it, Harriet?
Student 2:	Here is a puddle to splish and splash in, good for giving your shoes a wash in.
All:	Can you carry it, Harriet?
Student 3:	Here is a nest, snug in the straw, with warm, brown eggs, 1, 2, 3, 4.
All:	Can you carry it, Harriet?
Student 4:	Here comes Harriet's good friend Sue. Let's ask her what we can do.
Student 5:	Scoop the puddle up in a bucket. Now you can carry it, Harriet.
Student 1:	Catch the bee in a little jar. Now you can carry it, Harriet.
Student 2:	Put the nest of eggs in a basket. Now you can carry it, Harriet.
Student 3:	Take the bucket and water the plants.
Student 4:	Open the jar and free the bee.
Student 5:	Take just one egg carefully.
All:	Yes, you can carry it, Harriet.

Teaching Aids and References for Readers' Theater

Browse the web for sites that have scripts for Readers' Theater. Here are a few to visit:

Aaron Shepard's RT Page

http://www.aaronshep.com/rt/RTE.html

International Readers' theater (publish-on-demand script service)

http://www.cdli.ca/CITE/langrt.htm

Readers' Theater Scripts and Plays for the Classroom

http://teachingheart.net/readerstheater.htm

ReadingLady.com

http://cpanel.servdns.net/~readingl/Readers_Theater/Scripts/scripts.html

Storycart Press

www.storycart.com

Cecil, N. L., & Gipe, J. P. (2003). *Literacy in the intermediate grades: Best practices for a comprehensive program.* Scottsdale, AZ: Holcomb Hathaway, Publishers.

Diaz-Rico, L. T. (2004). *Teaching English learners: Strategies and methods.* Boston, MA: Pearson.

Hadaway, N. L., Vardell, S. M., & Young, T. A. (2002). *Literature-based instruction with English language learners, K–12.* Boston, MA: Allyn & Bacon.

Peregoy, S. F., & Boyle, O. F. (2005). *Reading, writing, and learning in ESL: A resource book for K–12 teachers.* Boston, MA: Pearson.

Sloyer, S. (1982). *Readers' theatre: Story dramatization in the classroom.* Urbana, IL: National Council of Teachers of English.

Walker, B. J. (1996). *Diagnostic teaching of reading: Techniques for instruction and assessment.* Columbus, OH: Merrill.

Children's Book References

Buxton, J. (1989) *Can you carry it, Harriet?* Auckland, NZ: Rigby.

Kessler, L. (1985). *The worst team ever.* New York: Dell.

CHORAL READING

Along with providing practice in fluent reading, choral reading also helps build self-confidence while students work as part of a group, and it promotes an appreciation for oral expression (Tierney, Readence, & Dishner, 1995). There are different formats with which to use choral reading (Tompkins, 2001). In echo reading, the group repeats each line after the leader. In small-group reading, each group is assigned a different part of the text to read. In cumulative reading, one group begins and others join in as they move through the text. The leader-and-chorus format lends itself to poetry and songs; a leader reads the main part, and the group reads the recurrent verse.

The Power of Choral Reading for Struggling Readers

- As a member of a group, struggling readers can increase confidence by taking chances without the threat of embarrassing corrections (Tierney, Readence, & Dishner, 1995).
- Supported by the group structure, struggling readers can make guesses with less chance of failure (Moffett & Wagner, 1992).

Steps to Follow

1. Choose a selection for the choral reading and either provide individual copies or write it on a large chart for all to see. The rhythm and flow of poetry and lyrics make them preferable texts to use for choral reading (Moffett & Wagner, 1992).
2. Read the text as a whole group several times.
3. Decide how to arrange the selection for reading. The copies or the chart can be color-coded or marked in some way so that students will know which section is theirs to read.
4. Decide together on specific intonations for individual words or lines.
5. Provide time for the students to practice.
6. Audiotape the reading and play it back for the group to discuss what changes or improvements need to be made.
7. Arrange for the students to share the reading with an audience.

Using Choral Reading with English Language Learners

Students of all ages will enjoy the choral reading of text from kindergartners' familiar poems and songs to middle and high school students' rhymes and raps of content area material. Choral reading is especially beneficial with ELL students (McCauley & McCauley, 1992). Because choral reading incorporates a low-anxiety environment with repeated practice, comprehensible input, and drama, it is an invaluable tool to use with English language learners. In addition to the previously listed steps to follow, look for selections of poems with action words; and then use gestures, postures, and stressed letters or syllables to clarify the meanings of the words. For those struggling readers who are making their way through the preprimer and primer stages, many traditional folk songs and tales can be found in leveled books by a variety of publishers.

Using Choral Reading to Improve Writing

As with Readers' Theater, a natural progression from using poems and other texts is for students to write their own scripts for performance. They might start by mimicking their favorite poetic structures or creating new or alternative verses for poems they already know. Another place to start would be with wordless picture books. The students could write the story as they see it through the pictures. Once the reading-writing connection is made and students are creating their own texts to perform, they will be improving their literacy competence in reading, writing, listening, and speaking.

Application and Examples

Try using poems for two voices as a link to writing. Finney (2003) discussed the use of this poetic structure to build critical literacy. Many of these poems reveal one perspective on one side/voice with an opposing perspective on the other. Once students have become very familiar with the format, they can begin writing their own poems for two voices.

To model the strategy, write a poem with your class, having one side be the teacher's point of view and the other side the students' opinions. Some topics to begin with could be homework, report cards, classroom rules, and so forth. From there, the students could go on to create many collaborative poems on topics of their interests and opinions.

Dottie and some third graders wrote a poem for two voices. One of the activities they engaged in was trading sides of the poem, with the students chorally reading the teacher's side and Dottie reading the students' side. Although this is great fun for the students, Finney (2003) pointed out that this gives students the opportunity to speak and listen to ideas that are different from their own: "The repeated reading of the poem offers multiple experiences with, and responses to, the same text as the students hear themselves speak both sides" (p. 75).

Homework

Homework. I love it!	Homework.
	I hate it!
I love it!	
	I hate it!
I love it! I do. I hand out the packets on Monday.	I hate it! I do.
	I open the packet on Thursday.
Homework! There's spelling.	Homework!
	Write a sentence for every word.

There's math.	
	Lots of problems.
Addition.	Addition.
Subtraction.	Subtraction.
Multiplication.	Multiplication.
My favorite!	My worst!
Homework.	
	Homework.
There's reading.	
Their choice of books.	My choice of books.
Number of minutes.	
Thirty.	Twenty.
Homework.	Homework.
There's writing.	
A story.	
	A letter.
A journal.	
	I'm done.
I can't wait until Friday.	I can't wait until Friday.
To see it turned in.	To get it turned in.
Now, I have the weekend.	Now, I have the weekend.
To read and grade it all.	
	To watch TV, to run, and play ball.
Yes Homework!	No Homework!

From teacher/student-generated poems, students can began working together as partners, in small groups, or on their own. At this point, they should begin to develop their own, more personal topics. Dottie approached her 8-year-old grandson to see if he would be willing to co-author a poem for two voices about a very personal recent event in his life. Following is the result of their collaboration:

Second Grade Spelling Bee

Spelling Bee.	Spelling Bee.
Whose idea was this?	
	I'm a great speller.
Week after week.	
	I spelled them all right.
Word after word.	
	I'm on a roll.
Elimination.	Elimination.
	Not me.
Down to three.	I'm one of three.
Going to the finals.	
	Going to the finals.
Parents invited.	

Words are in baskets.

Spelling Bee.
Easy, Medium, Hard.

Make.
Some.
Medium.

String.
Strong.
Hard.

Spelling Bee.
Woman: A woman went to the store.

Rule is start over, new word.

Because.
Beautiful.
Spelling Bee.

Believe.

Yes.

Sorry, please sit down.
Spelling Bee.

Mom, Dad, Grandma, too.

Ready to go.
Spelling Bee.

Start with easy.
M-A-K-E.
S-O-M-E.

I'm ready.
S-T-R-I-N-G.
S-T-R-O-N-G.

Let's move on.
Spelling Bee.

W-O-M-E-N.
Three kids in a row spelled it wrong.

Still in the Bee.
B-E-C-A-U-S-E.
B-E-A-U-T-I-F-U-L.

Spelling Bee.

I can't believe . . .
May I start again?

I can't believe.
I forgot the "i" in believe.
Spelling Bee.
Next year!

Teaching Aids and References for Choral Reading

The following list of outstanding poets is a starting place for gathering children's poetry for your classroom and your students' choral reading. The first 10 poets on the list have won the National Council of Teachers of English (NCTE) Award for Excellence in Poetry for Children. This award is given to living poets for exceptional quality in a body of work (not just one book or poem) for ages 3 to 13 (Temple, Martinez, Yokota, & Naylor, 1998):

1. David McCord
2. Aileen Fisher
3. Karla Kuskin
4. Myra Cohn Livingston
5. Arnold Adoff
6. Eve Merriam
7. John Ciardi
8. Lilian Moore
9. Valerie Worth
10. Barbara Juster Esbensen
11. Jack Prelutsky
12. Shel Silverstein
13. Nikki Giovanni
14. Langston Hughes
15. A. A. Milne
16. Walter de la Mare
17. Robert Louis Stevenson
18. Lee Bennett Hopkins

As discussed earlier, poems for two voices are excellent sources for choral reading selections. Two of Paul Fleischman's titles are *I Am Phoenix: Poems for Two Voices* and *Joyful Noise: Poems for Two Voices*. For doubling the effort and enjoyment, there is Fleischman's *Big Talk: Poems for Four Voices*. Also, look for leveled books written for primer and preprimer readers that lend themselves to rhythmic choral reading:

Title	Publisher
1. *Can You Carry It, Harriet?*	Rigby
2. *Catch the Cookie*	Scott Foresman
3. *Down by the Bay*	Scott Foresman
4. *Here We Go Round the Mulberry Bush*	Houghton Mifflin
5. *On Top of Spaghetti*	Scott Foresman

Finney, M. J. (2003). A bumper sticker, Columbus, and a poem for two voices. *The Reading Teacher, 57*(1), 74–77.

McCauley, J. K., & McCauley, D. S. (1992). Using choral reading to promote language learning for ELL students. *The Reading Teacher, 45,* 526–533.

Moffett, J., & Wagner, B. J. (1992). *Student-centered language arts K–12.* Portsmouth, NH: Boynton/Cook Publishers.

Temple, C., Martinez, M., Yokota, J., & Naylor, A. (1998). *Children's books in children's hands.* Boston: Allyn & Bacon.

Tierney, R. J., Readence, J. E., & Dishner, E. K. (1995). *Reading strategies and practices: A compendium.* Boston: Allyn & Bacon.

Tompkins, G. E. (2001). *Literacy for the twenty-first century: A balanced approach.* Upper Saddle River, NJ: Merrill/Prentice Hall.

Children's Book References

Buxton, J. (1989). *Can you carry it, Harriet?* Crystal Lake, IL: Rigby.

Buxton, J. (1993). *Down by the bay.* Glenview, IL: Scott Foresman and Company.

Fleischman, P. (1985). *I am Phoenix: Poems for two voices.* New York: Harper & Row.

Fleischman, P. (1988). *Joyful noise: Poems for two voices.* New York: Harper & Row.

Fleischman, P. (2000). *Big talk: Poems for four voices.* Cambridge, MA: Candlewick Press.

Glazer, T. (1993). *On top of spaghetti.* Glenview, IL: Scott Foresman and Company.

Glazer, T. (1995). *Here we go round the mulberry bush.* Boston: Houghton Mifflin.

Vaughn, M. (1996). *Catch the cookie.* Glenview, IL: Scott Foresman and Company.

LISTENING TO TEXT

The reading of stories to students has long been an accepted and expected practice in classrooms. The oral reading of text by skilled readers provides a model of how the text should "sound" for inexperienced readers. The fluent reading, in turn, enhances the comprehension of the text for listeners. Even adults who are capable readers may need a skilled model to fully comprehend a text that uses unusual sentence structure or antiquated language.

Consider, for example, the text of a Shakespearean play. Unless you are an English teacher who regularly teaches Shakespeare, chances are you will comprehend the text more fully by hearing it recited by skilled actors while you follow along with the text. This is exactly what many high school teachers and university professors do to help students understand Shakespeare. (Of course, seeing and hearing the play performed is the ultimate comprehension experience!)

Listening and its relationship to reading has been a topic for research in the past (see Weiss, 1978, for a summary of early research). Lundsteen (1979) concluded after extensive research that listening is the process that allows spoken language to be converted to meaning in the mind. Many teachers, unfortunately, assume that listening is a matter of paying attention and often neglect this area of language ability. Listening comprehension is used as an estimate of students' reading potential because the listening comprehension of children surpasses their reading comprehension until about seventh grade (Sticht & Beck, 1976, in Gipe, 1995).

More recently, listening to books on tape has been used successfully with second language learners in a home-school shared reading program (Blum et al., 1998). "Repeated reading with an auditory model provides critical support—scaffolding which enables these novices to feel like expert readers. This initial success provides confidence and strong motivation to practice, which is essential to develop skilled, fluent readers" (Blum et al., 1998, p. 5).

The Power of Listening to Text for Struggling Readers

Struggling readers who need to improve fluency can become successful by following along and listening to text read by a skilled reader. Following are some of the benefits:

- Demonstration of proper phasing and intonation assists in comprehension.

- Incorporation of listening to text on audiotapes and CDs into classroom literacy programs allows struggling readers to see this activity as part of the learning process for all students and does not cause them to feel singled out.

- Integration of this strategy as a piece of the Language Arts block of instruction allows students to work independently for an extended period of time while building struggling readers' self-confidence.

Steps to Follow

1. Consider the quality of the work, as with any book selection, along with the interests and abilities of the readers. A good rule of thumb for students who will listen to a book in their first language is that the book be one year above their reading level. In general, classroom teachers need a wide range of recorded book levels just as they do for other books in their classroom library.

2. Use audio books that indicate to readers when to turn the page for very young readers or for second language learners who may not have one-to-one correspondence with oral language and print.

3. Enlist other skilled student readers from other grades, parents, or volunteers to record books from the classroom collection, if resources are limited.

4. Guide struggling readers to listen to books that gradually increase in difficulty. Predictable patterned books and books that repeat high-frequency words are a good place to start. Based on individual needs, a list of listening books for the week can be given to each child.

5. Help students understand the purpose for listening to the recorded books. Most students enjoy a listening activity but may not intuitively know how following along with a reader will improve their own reading skills.

6. Encourage students to listen to a story several times but with slightly different purposes each time: the first time may be to be able to maintain voice-to-word correspondence; the second time may be to learn new sight words; a third time may be to attend to the reader's phrasing, and so on.

Using Listening to Text with English Language Learners

English learners should be provided with many opportunities throughout the day to practice and use reading, writing, listening, and speaking: effective teachers understand the four language processes are mutually supportive and interdependent. "Practice in any one promotes development in the others" (Echevarria, Vogt, & Short, 2004, p. 120). Listening and reading are receptive uses of language, but they are not passive processes (Peregoy & Boyle, 2005). Increased listening comprehension leads to increased reading comprehension because listeners must actively recreate the speaker's message in order to understand it.

Using Listening to Text to Improve Writing

Many writing activities may evolve from listening to text. Ask students to provide short answers to questions about the story or to write a personal response. Students may keep listening journals in which they respond to or summarize different listening events during the week (Diaz-Rico, 2004). As Peregoy and Boyle (2005) pointed out, reading, writing, listening, and speaking are naturally integrated in our daily activities. It is natural for us to talk to someone about a newspaper article, a letter, e-mail, or any number of other pieces of writing. As students participate in these types of activities in the classroom, they are experiencing the natural integration of the language processes, and they are growing in all four.

Application and Examples

As with the repeated reading strategy, repeated listening to the same text will increase reading fluency. At the Paradise Professional Development School, listening centers are established in most classrooms. All students in the second grade visit the classroom listening center twice a week. Students who have been identified as needing additional fluency development listen to text three or four times a week. Dottie helped the teachers develop a way for these students to keep track of their purposes for listening to books on tape as shown in Figure 4.1 (see Appendix for Form 5).

Teaching Aids and References for Listening to Text

Children's books on tape and CDs can be found easily in places ranging from supermarkets to the Internet. Quality varies, however, and

Name _____

Title of book _____

Author _____

First time listening: Date completed _____

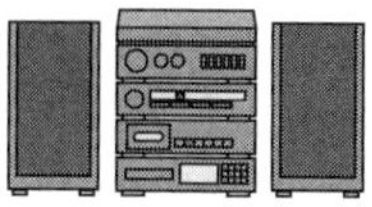

Listen to the story. Follow along with the reader. Enjoy the story.

Second time listening: Date completed _____

Listen to the story. Try to read the words with the reader.

Third time listening: Date completed _____

Listen to the story again and try to become the reader. Then read the book or a favorite part to someone.

FIGURE 4.1   Listening Center Activities.

may require some research before making purchases. Some audio books are not the exact text or have been abridged in some way. We suggest that you purchase audio tapes or CD sets that come with the books rather than the tape or CD independently from the books. If the main purpose of having students listen to text is to improve their fluency, make sure that the recorded versions do not have so many "sound effects" as to distract from that purpose.

There are several helpful websites that provide reviews and comments about children's books on tape. Great Tapes for Kids (www.greattapes.com) and Audio Books on Compact Discs, Inc. (www.abcdinc.com) are two sites that provide useful information. For online listening and short quiz responses, direct your students to Randall's Listening Lab at www.esl-lab.com.

Professional References

Blum, I., Koskinen, P., Tennant, T., Parker, E. M., Straub, M., & Curry, C. (1998). *Ongoing research: Have you heard any good books lately? Using audiotaped books to extend classroom literacy instruction into the homes of second-language learners.* NRRC, 1998, pp. 4–5.

Diaz-Rico, L. T. (2004). *Teaching English learners: Strategies and methods.* Boston, MA: Pearson.

Echevarria, J., Vogt, M., & Short, D. J. (2004). *Making content comprehensible for English learners: The SIOP model.* Boston, MA: Pearson.

Gipe, J. (1995). *Corrective reading techniques for classroom teachers.* Scottsdale, AZ: Gorsuch Scarisbrick.

Lundsteen, S. (1979). *Listening: Its impact on reading and other language arts* (rev. ed.). Urbana, IL: National Council of Teachers.

Peregoy, S. F., & Boyle, O. F. (2005). *Reading, writing, and learning in ESL: A resource book for K–12 teachers.* Boston, MA: Pearson.

Weiss, M. J. (1978). Listening: The neglected communication skill. In Patrick J. Finn & Walter T. Petty (Eds.), *Facilitating language development* (pp. 108–114). Amherst, NY: SUNYAB.

WORKING WITH MIDDLE SCHOOL STUDENTS TO IMPROVE FLUENCY: CONNECTING REREADING TO NOTE-TAKING

As students move into middle school their texts become increasingly more difficult. Some students, who may have been confident, fluent readers in elementary school, find they are reading more slowly, with less accuracy, or with less confidence (Cecil & Gipe, 2003). The repeated reading strategy will benefit middle school students as well as it does struggling elementary or ELL students. The use of audiotapes for content area material could be helpful for middle school students experiencing difficulty with their expository textbooks (Sadler, 2001). Audiotapes could be purchased as ancillary materials that accompany content textbooks, or perhaps volunteers would be willing to record parts of the text. Students could then check out the audiotapes for home rereading.

The rereading strategy can be combined with note-taking practice, making the reading-writing connection. Following mini-lessons from the teacher, students can use nonfiction trade books and textbooks to practice note-taking (Hadaway, Vardell, & Young, 2002). As they reread texts, they can practice their note-taking skills and then go on to rewording and paraphrasing the information they've acquired. As they practice this procedure, they will be learning to listen to longer and longer instructional segments, preparing them for much of the lecture-style instruction they will receive in high school and college.

The Power of Connecting Rereading to Note-Taking

With the departmentalization structure in middle or junior high schools, students may see each of their content areas as separate and unrelated entities. The benefits of connecting rereading and note-taking include the following:

- Linking Language Arts skills and strategies to learning in content-area classrooms provides coherence.
- Increased competence in any of the language processes has a positive influence on the others.

Steps to Follow

1. Play an audiotape of content-area material, modeling note-taking strategies.
2. Model using the notes to reword or paraphrase the key points.
3. Using a different audiotape, have students practice the note-taking strategies.
4. Compare and discuss note-taking results.
5. Direct students to practice writing a summary of key points from their notes.
6. Encourage students to check out content-area audiotapes to reread and practice note-taking and paraphrasing.

Teaching Aids and References for Improving Fluency Connecting Rereading to Note-Taking

Check with publishers to see if audiotapes from content areas are available as complements to the text. Ask volunteers or older students to tape chapters or sections of expository text.

Professional References

Cecil, N. L., & Gipe, J. P. (2003). *Literacy in the intermediate grades: Best practices for a comprehensive program.* Scottsdale, AZ: Holcomb Hathaway, Publishers.

Hadaway, N. L., Vardell, S. M., & Young, T. A. (2002). *Literature-based instruction with English language learners, K–12.* Boston, MA: Allyn & Bacon.

Sadler, C. R. (2001). *Comprehension strategies for middle grade learners: A handbook for content area teachers.* Newark, DE: International Reading Association.

Assessing Fluency

As we discussed previously, we want our struggling readers to decode text automatically, allowing them to concentrate more on meaning. It is important to note, however, that assessment of fluency is not assessment of

comprehension. Dottie has been working with a second-grade English
language learner, who is a very fluent reader at a beginning first-grade level.
When assessing his fluency, she finds that he makes relatively few miscues,
reading with 96% accuracy. However, her student can tell her little of what
he reads. When asked to do a retelling, his comprehension of a fluently read
passage is found to be extremely low. Even when prompted with leading
questions, he cannot provide the literal meaning of the text. This is our
caution: remember that fluency may lead to increased comprehension, but it
does not necessarily indicate that comprehension is present.

Earlier, we described the strategy of repeated reading and provided a
graph that can be used to chart progress. The assessment graph can be
kept by the teacher, but the student may also keep one as a form of self-
assessment. Using the repeated reading graph provides students with a
self-assessment that represents their progress as well as their goals.

The strategies of listening to text can be combined with recording of
text to be used as a teacher assessment or student self-assessment. After
students have listened to an audiotape of a selection and they feel
confident in their own reading of the passage, they can record it at the
listening center. Then they can play it back as a form of self-assessment
and provide the teacher with a copy of the tape. Some teachers have the
students record themselves periodically throughout the year. The tapes
can be played for classroom assessment or sent home for play by the
parents and then added to the students' literacy portfolios.

Many informal reading inventories provide fluency assessments for
the passages in the form of miscue analysis protocols. The one most
frequently used at the Literacy Development Center and at the Paradise
Professional Development School is *Reading Inventory for the Classroom*
(Flynt & Cooter, 2000). As the authors of the inventory note, once a
student has been unable to answer three or more of the silent reading
comprehension questions, no higher-level passages should be attempted.
This ties into our earlier discussion of students who may read with few
miscues but have little comprehension.

Another assessment that can be used to monitor fluency progress is
the running record (Clay, 1993). A running record is a word-by-word
written recording of a student's oral reading of a selection. For each word
read correctly, a tick is made on a blank piece of paper. Several shorthand
conventions are used to record errors. Clay provides a conversion chart to
simplify the determination of accuracy levels upon completion of a
running record. When first attempting running records, teachers
sometimes find it difficult to keep up with the reader and/or to record the
errors. However, with some practice, it becomes easier. Running records
provide a quick, concise, visual assessment of a student's fluency.

Professional References

Clay, M. M. (1993). *An observation survey for early literacy achievement.*
    Portsmouth, NH: Heinemann.
Flynt, E. S., & Cooter, R. B., Jr. (2000). *Reading inventory for the classroom.*
    Upper Saddle River, NJ: Merrill/Prentice Hall.

PART V

When Struggling Readers and Writers Need to Improve Comprehension

There are times when even the best readers have difficulty understanding a text. Comprehension difficulties may occur for many reasons; some may arise when there is a mismatch between author and reader. A reader may fail to understand a given text because the author (a) uses unfamiliar vocabulary and/or complex sentence structures, and (b) discusses topics or ideas for which the reader has no prior knowledge or experiences. General factors such as reader interest and motivation, as well as lack of understanding of the reading process, also affect comprehension.

Some students do well in reading until they begin to read more content area materials such as science and social studies texts. These students are very comfortable with narrative text, but they are unfamiliar with the overall structure of expository text. For other students, comprehension problems may be seen when they are asked to think critically or to make inferences about the text.

The following strategies provide a variety of ways to enhance students' understanding of text.

RETELLING

Retelling is an excellent strategy to build comprehension skills. "Retelling is grounded in an understanding of the crucial role that oral language plays in both the formation and sharing of meaning" (Gambrell, Koskinen, & Kapinus, 1991). Retelling is a strategy that can be used with students in all grade levels. Students can retell a story one-on-one with the teacher, with a peer partner, or in a small group. Through retelling, you can help students organize ideas, focus on important details, and incorporate new vocabulary into their oral language.

The Power of Retelling for Struggling Readers

- By concentrating on the story elements, students gain in-depth understanding of the text. Students learn to examine key components of literary elements and genres which leads to improved comprehension and enhanced enjoyment of the text.

- Students reveal what they remember as well as what they understand through retelling.

- Practice in retelling contributes to improved comprehension in both proficient and less-proficient readers (Gambrell, Koskinen, & Kapinus, 1991; Bensen & Cummins, 1999).

- Retelling also helps learners internalize information and concepts, such as vocabulary and story structure (Brown & Cambourne, 1987).

Steps to Follow

1. Model a retelling. Read aloud a story, stopping from time to time, to plan aloud what information will be included in the retelling. For example, when retelling a traditional version of Cinderella, you might say: "I know when I retell this story I want to make sure I tell how Cinderella came to live with her stepmother and stepsisters."

   When the reading of the selection is finished, retell it to the students, asking them to listen for important details.

2. Let the students know that they will be asked to retell a story as if to a friend who has never heard it before. Explain to the students what is expected in the retelling of the story with a story guide (see Figures 5.1A and B): characters, setting, plot with main episodes, and resolution. Depending on grade level, you may want to modify the language used for the story guide: who is in the story, when did it happen, what happened, how does it end?

3. Have the students read and retell the story.

4. Allow students to use puppets, story boards, or other props during the retelling.

5. If students have difficulty retelling the story, prompt with questions: What happened in the beginning? Where did the story take place? What happened next? How was the problem solved? How did the story end?

6. If important details of the story have been omitted in the retelling, ask specific questions or refer the student back to the text to reread excluded sections.

Using Retelling with English Language Learners

The telling of stories is a component of most cultures' oral traditions. With ELL students, building the connection between telling a story orally in their native language and then retelling in English is extremely helpful.

To begin developing skills related to retelling, you can ask students to exchange oral histories. Students can tell about an event in their personal lives to a peer either in English or their native language, such as what happened at a birthday party or how it was beginning the year at a new school. The student who heard the personal story then retells it to a third student while the original storyteller listens. The original storyteller then comments on the accuracy of the retelling: "Yes, you told all the parts of my story" or "You forgot the part about. . . ."

From the oral histories, you can use wordless picture books to generate the storylines. Students can rely on the story structure that the pictures provide and orally tell a story in English or their native language. There are many wordless picture books available (see references); you will want to select these books as carefully as you select other books for their students.

Using Retelling to Improve Writing

Oral retelling leads logically to written retelling. The story guides suggested can provide struggling writers with the support they may need to transition from oral to written language. In addition, wordless picture books can be an excellent support for students who may struggle with creating their own stories. Many wordless picture books contain the literary elements we look for in texts such as point of view, theme, character development, and setting.

You might start with a relatively simple story such as any of the Mercer Mayer titles and encourage students to "read" the book completely before they begin to write. Once the students have a sense of the story, encourage them to orally provide a sentence or two for each page. As they "tell" the story, you can either act as a scribe or use a tape recorder. If you choose the latter, the students can then replay the tape to transform their oral tale to written form. Struggling writers will likely be successful working with partners as they retell the story from wordless picture books. They can also work with small groups, with students alternating the roles of storyteller and scribe.

Application and Example

Retelling can be further extended by using a variety of story guides. Two examples of story guides often used in elementary classrooms are made with a 12×18 sheet of white construction paper.

1.   Beginning, middle, and end (see Figure 5.1A).

Fold the piece of construction paper lengthwise. On the front half only, make two slits from the edge to the fold, creating three equal sections. Label these: Beginning, Middle, and End. After opening up the construction paper story guide, students then write a brief sentence and draw an illustration for each labeled part of the story.

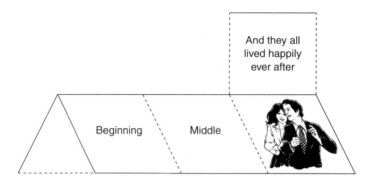

FIGURE 5.1A   Retelling Story Guide.

FIGURE 5.1B   Retelling Story Guide.

2.   Characters, setting, plot, and solution (see Figure 5.1B).

Fold a piece of construction paper lengthwise. Only on the front piece, make three slits from the edge to the fold to create four equal sections. Label these: Characters, Setting, Plot, and Solution. After opening up the construction paper story guide, students then write a brief sentence and draw an illustration for each labeled part of the story.

One of Dottie's undergraduate teacher education students, Diane, incorporated retelling into her tutoring of a third grader, Danny, over a two-month period. Diane followed the basic plan for retelling as stated in "Steps to Follow." Once Danny was comfortable with retelling, Diane had him use the story guides to demonstrate his comprehension of independently read stories. Diane also enhanced Danny's understanding of the reading-writing connection by having him write each of the retellings. Diane then wordprocessed each of the retellings to be included in the child's portfolio. At the end of the tutoring sessions, Diane proudly shared Danny's portfolio with the other preservice teachers. Over nine sessions, Diane was able to guide Danny from one sentence in their initial session to a full-page retelling in their last session. When Diane shared Danny's progress with his teacher, the classroom teacher commented that Danny had become "quite the storyteller" by the end of the tutoring sessions.

Teaching Aids and References for Retelling

Bensen, V., & Cummins, C. (1999) *The power of retelling: Developmental steps for building comprehension.* Bothell, WA: The Wright Group.

Brown, H., & Cambourne, B. (1987). *Read and retell: A strategy for the whole-langugage/natural learning classroom.* Portsmouth, NH: Heinemann.

Cooper, P. (1993). *When stories come to school: Telling, writing, and performing stories in the early childhood classroom.* New York: Teachers & Writers Collaborative.

Gambrell, L. B., & Dromsky, A. (2000). Fostering reading comprehension. In D. S. Strickland & L. M. Morrow (Eds.), *Beginning reading and writing* (pp. 145–153). Newark, DE: International Reading Association, & New York: Teachers College Press, Columbia University.

Gambrell, L. B., Koskinen, P. S., & Kapinus, B. A. (1991). Retelling and the reading comprehension of proficient and less-proficient readers. *Journal of Educational Research, 84*(6), 356–362.

Morrow, L. M. (1985). Retelling stories: A strategy for improving young children's comprehension, concept of story structure, and oral language complexity. *Elementary School Journal, 85*(5), 647–661.

National Reading Panel. (2000). *Report of the National Reading Panel. Teaching children to read: An evidence-based assessment of the scientific research literature on reading and its implications for reading instruction.* Washington, DC: National Institute of Child Health and Human Development.

Children's Wordless Picture Books

See the following websites for current wordless book titles:

University of Illinois at Urbana-Champaign
http://door.library.uiuc.edu/edx/wordless.htm

Slippery Rock University
http://www.sru.edu/pages/5965.asp

University of Wisconsin-Madison
http://www.education.wisc.edu/ccbc/bibs/40books/wordless.htm

BREAKING DOWN THE TEXT

When students listen to and read good literature as part of their literacy development, they meet authors who use real language in real ways. The texts tell engaging stories or present interesting facts written with sentence structure that may be very different from students' own speech patterns as well as the structure used in early basal readers or leveled books. Through the oral reading of good literature to students, you can develop students' listening comprehension of texts with complex sentence structures and less common language patterns. As listeners, students are often drawn to these texts just because of the novel language patterns used by the authors. These texts may challenge readers to make sense of the author's message and require modeling and explanation from skilled teachers. "Breaking down the text" is a strategy through which you can show students how to make complex text more simple and understandable.

The Power of Breaking Down the Text for Struggling Readers

- The strategy leads to independence in reading comprehension because it allows students to understand how complex and lengthy sentences can be broken down into more manageable parts.
- Students learn to understand an author's style of writing.
- Students will write more complex sentences in their own compositions.

Steps to Follow

1. Select a paragraph from a student's book, textbook, or newspaper in which the author uses complex sentence structures and a variety of punctuation. Text that is at a small group's "too hard" level is appropriate.

2. Reproduce the paragraph for the students and prepare a copy of the paragraph for use on the overhead projector. Leave spacing between lines of print so words and phrases may be underlined, circled, and so on.

3. Read the selection to the students. Ask the students to follow along and be ready to find sentences, words, and punctuation.

4. Following your model, have the students number the sentences.

5. Through modeling and questioning, help students to see how the author has put together small, related thought units into one sentence. Note the author's use of punctuation to accomplish this way of writing. An example of this is in the Application and Example section.

6. Have students work with a partner and try to break down the text of another paragraph from the same book or article.

Using the Strategy of Breaking Down the Text with English Language Learners

"Breaking down the text" can be used with English language learners in a similar way as previously described. Carefully select text so that the sentence and text structures support comprehension rather than confound it, especially when oral English proficiency is still developing for students. Fitzgerald (1995) suggests that passages organized in familiar structures are easier for second language learners to comprehend that are passages with unusual or novel text structures. Comprehension for second language learners is enhanced through "breaking down the text" by focusing on the vocabulary, syntax, and rhetorical structures of a text.

Improving Writing by Breaking Down the Text

Through "breaking down the text," struggling readers are shown how to simplify a complex text so that they can more easily comprehend an author's message. Ultimately, however, we want students to understand that it is the complexity of the text that makes the message meaningful. We also want students to understand that they are capable of writing complex text just like real authors.

Killgallon and Killgallon (2000) take this approach to improving writing. By using "real" sentences from students' stories and novels as models, they introduce four sentence-manipulating techniques: sentence unscrambling, sentence imitating, sentence combining, and sentence expanding. By playing with these sentences, students write their own sentences in more effective and interesting ways (see Figure 5.2A).

Application and Example

Sarah, a third grader, attended the Literacy Development Center for an after-school program. During her initial interview with her tutor, she revealed that she wanted to be able to read the books that Patty, one of her friends, reads. "She's a very good reader," Sarah told Juanita. When Sarah and Juanita visited the Center's library to select a book to take home for the week, Sarah found *Stuart Little* by E. B. White (Harper & Row, 1945). "This is what I want to read. Patty read this!" Sarah declared.

Based on Sarah's informal assessment results, Juanita suggested that this book be one of Sarah's challenge books that they could work on together during her tutoring time. Sarah said she wanted to take the book home and try it. Juanita discussed the plan with Sarah's mother and asked if she would work with Sarah on Chapters 1 and 2.

After sharing *The Polar Express* by Chris Van Allsburg with students, teachers can model how to imitate an author by doing a think-aloud. For example:
Let's look at one of Allsburg's sentences:

"We climbed mountains so high it seemed as if we would scrape the moon."

When I read this sentence, I really get the feeling that the Polar Express is traveling up very high mountains. Allsburg used the phrase "scrape the moon" to help me feel that way. I can write a sentence like this one if I think about what it would be like traveling during the night. I would see the moon and I would see the stars. Allsburg used the "scrape" to give the feeling of coming so close to the moon that the train would rub across it. I'm going to try a sentence:

"We climbed mountains so high it seemed as if we would **touch the stars.**"
Does my sentence give you the same feeling as Allsburg's?

Let's see if you can write a sentence like Allsburg did. Remember when the train awoke the boy? Allsburg wrote:

"It was wrapped in an apron of steam." You probably have seen someone wear an apron when cooking. Now try writing this sentence your way.

FIGURE 5.2A Write It Your Way.

Stuart was an early riser: he was almost always the first person up in the morning. He liked the feeling of being the first one stirring; he enjoyed the quiet rooms with the books standing still on the shelves, the pale light coming in through the windows, and the fresh smell of day. In wintertime it would be quite dark when he climbed from his bed made out of the cigarette box, and he sometimes shivered with cold as he stood in his nightgown doing his exercises. (Stuart touched his toes ten times every morning to keep himself in good condition. He had seen his brother George do it, and George had explained that it kept his stomach muscles firm and was a fine abdominal thing to do.)

FIGURE 5.2B   Excerpt from *Stuart Little* by E. B. White for "Breaking Down the Text."

①
STUART was an early riser: he was almost always the first person up in the
                      ②
morning. He liked the feeling of being the first one stirring; he enjoyed the

quiet rooms with the books standing still on the shelves, the pale light coming
                                                  ③
in through the windows, and the fresh smell of day. In wintertime it would be

quite dark when he climbed from his bed made out of the cigarette box, and

he sometimes shivered with cold as he stood in his nightgown doing his
               ④
exercises. (Stuart touched his toes ten times every morning to keep himself
                   ⑤
in good condition. He had seen his brother George do it, and George had

explained that it kept his stomach muscles firm and was a fine abdominal

thing to do.)

FIGURE 5.2C   Working Copy for "Breaking Down the Text."

When Sarah returned the following week, she told Juanita that she had read the first two chapters with her mother but needed "a lot of help because the sentences were so long." Juanita had a copy of the first page of Chapter 3 ready and began to teach Sarah how to break down text (Figures 5.2B and 5.2C).

Juanita: This is a copy of the first page of Chapter 3. I'm going to show you how you can better understand this author using a strategy called "breaking down the text." The first thing we need to do is number the sentences. Let's put a number in the beginning of each sentence. How many sentences do you find? (Sarah proceeded to number the sentences. When she got to the parentheses at the beginning of sentence 4, she stopped.)

Sarah: Is this a sentence? Why is this mark here?

Juanita: Have you seen it before?

Sarah: No.

Juanita:	That is called a parenthesis and they come in pairs. One is open to the right and one is open to the left. Let's underline them. Can you find the other one?
Sarah:	Okay, there it is.
Juanita:	Now if we look inside the parentheses, we find two more sentences. Number them.
Sarah:	There are five sentences all together.
Juanita:	Great. Now let's go back to the beginning. Let's read the first sentence together.
S and J:	*Stuart was an early riser: he was almost always the first person up in the morning.*
Juanita:	What can you tell me about Stuart?
Sarah:	He liked to get up early in the morning.
Juanita:	Anything else?
Sarah:	He is usually the first one up.
Juanita:	Can you find the colon in that sentence? Let's put a circle around it. (Sarah finds the colon and circles it.) Some authors might have put a period after the word *riser* and begun a new sentence with *he*. E. B. White didn't because he wanted the reader to know that the two ideas about Stuart are very much related. When an author uses a colon he wants the reader to pay attention to what is coming next. The first part of the sentence *Stuart was an early riser* introduces the next part *he was almost always the first person up in the morning.* The second part explains more about the first.
Sarah:	OK.
Juanita:	Let's read the second sentence together. *He liked the feeling of being the first one stirring; he enjoyed the quiet rooms with the books standing still on the shelves, the pale light coming in through the windows, and the fresh smell of day.* (Juanita noticed that Sarah hesitated with "stirring.") Let's look at the word *stirring*. I'm putting a box around it. Have you heard that word before?
Sarah:	Yeah, like when you stir soup.
Juanita:	That's right but that meaning doesn't fit here. Have you ever heard the poem: *Twas the night before Christmas, And all through the house, Not a creature was stirring, Not even a mouse?*
Sarah:	I know that poem.
Juanita:	Well, *stirring* in that poem has the meaning as in this sentence about Stuart.
Sarah:	And he *is* a mouse.
Juanita:	Right. So what does it mean?
Sarah:	It means moving around. Stuart liked to be the first one moving around the house when everyone else was still sleeping.

1. Try to work with just a small part of the text at a time.
2. Find the beginning and end of each sentence.
3. Read the first sentence. If it is a long sentence, look for commas, colons, and semicolons to help understand the parts of the sentence.
4. Read the next sentence. Think of how it connects to the first sentence.
5. Repeat these steps.

FIGURE 5.2D   Review Card for "Breaking Down the Text."

Juanita: Very good. Now let's look at the rest of the sentence. Do you see another punctuation mark? Circle it. (Sarah does.) That's a semicolon.

Juanita continued in this manner until they reached the end of the section. Then Juanita helped Sarah make a review card to keep nearby when she encountered text that was complex.

Teaching Aids and References on Breaking Down the Text

Figure 5.2D is a review card for breaking down the text. You may find it helpful to make a large poster of these steps for students to see when working on challenging text.

Activities for ESL students may be found at
http://a4esl.org/

Boyle, O., & Peregoy, S. (1990) Literacy scaffolds: Strategies for first and second language readers and writers. *The Reading Teacher, 44,*(3), 194–201.

Fitzgerald, J. (1995). English-as-a-second-language learner's cognitive processes: A review of research in the United States. *Review of Educational Research, 65,* 145–190.

Killgallon, D., & Killgallon, J. (2000). *Sentence composing for elementary school: A worktext to build better sentences.* Portsmouth, NH: Heinemann.

Snow, C. E., Burns, S. M., & Griffin, P. (Eds.). (1998). *Preventing reading difficulties in young children, executive summary.* National Research Council, National Academy of Sciences. Courtesy of National Academy Press.

Vavra, E. (1996). On not teaching grammar. *English Journal, 85*(7), 32–37.

UNDERSTANDING TEXT STRUCTURE

"Breaking down the text" can be used with narrative and expository text. Authors of expository text, however, write differently than authors of narrative text in the ways they organize their thoughts and communicate information to their readers. Expository text explains and informs the reader about topics, concepts, and ideas. Often these topics, concepts, and ideas are foreign to readers. This, coupled with the fact that expository text structure differs from narrative, makes expository text challenging for many students.

Learning in any content area, such as mathematics, science, and history, is primarily a matter of learning the language of the discipline. You need to instruct students in the vocabulary of the content area and the text structure that is characteristic of the field of study (Pinnell & Jagger, 1991). You can help students understand expository text structure through direct instruction of text structures.

There are basic expository text structures at the paragraph level that you can begin to teach to students. The seven most common text structures are: (a) enumeration, (b) description, (c) cause/effect, (d) time/order, (e) classification, (f) comparison/contrast, and (g) persuasion. In addition, instruction in the reading of hypertext is also necessary as more online texts are integrated into instruction and as students incorporate them into their reading selections. When reading a textbook, students usually read page by page in a linear fashion; they may skip or scan pages to locate information. With hypertext, readers can navigate freely through the text, even leaving the initial text to read something related. It is possible for different students, each beginning with the same hypertext, to have a completely different reading experience based on the many individual decisions that hypertext allows.

The Power of Understanding Text Structure for Struggling Readers

By helping struggling readers understand different text structures used by authors you:

■ Provide students with a way to understand the author's message through an understanding of how language is organized in a text.

■ Introduce key vocabulary words and phrases that help readers recognize the text structure and predict what will be next in the text. For example, "on the other hand" is a key phrase used by authors when comparing and contrasting topics, concepts, or ideas.

■ Assist students with their own writing as they learn more about what authors do with expository text. They learn how to read like a writer (Smith, 1983).

Steps to Follow

1. Select two common objects that are familiar to all students in your class or group (e.g., an apple and an orange).
2. Draw two overlapping circles (Venn Diagram) on the board or overhead projector.
3. Ask the students to brainstorm the characteristics of each object and list them on the areas of the circles that do not overlap.
4. Then ask the students to read the characteristics that both objects have in common. Write these in the overlapping area.
5. Present a short paragraph to the students that compares and contrasts the two objects. Read the paragraph to them and model using a "think-aloud" exercise on how to understand the text. Point out key words and phrases that signal the compare/contrast text structure.
6. Have the students look through science and social studies books to see if they can locate paragraphs in which the author uses the compare/contrast structure.
7. Ask the students to write about two objects of their choice in which they use the compare/contrast structure.
8. Working with a partner, have the students identify key words and phrases in their partners' paragraphs.

Using Understanding Text Structure with English Language Learners

Direct instruction in the vocabulary used in expository text is an important step in helping English language learners comprehend text structure. When working with limited English students, it is important to lay an oral language foundation before reading and writing.

For example, you can present vocabulary to help students understand time/order structure. Using the day's schedule and symbols from clip art or drawings to identify subject areas, you can "read" the schedule to the students (see Figure 5.3A):

This is today's schedule. First (Primero), we will have reading groups. Second (Segundo), we will go to PE. Third (Tercero), we will have science. Then (Entonces) we

First ⟶ Primero

Second ⟶ Segundo

Third ⟶ Tercero

Then ⟶ Entonces

After ⟶ Después

Finally ⟶ Finalmente

FIGURE 5.3A Time/Order Vocabulary.

will have lunch. After (Después) lunch, we will have math centers. Finally (Finalmente), we will write in our journals before we go home.

Then ask the students to use both the English and Spanish vocabulary orally before introducing a simple time/order written text.

Improving Writing Through Understanding Text Structure

Wray and Lewis (1998) suggest that writing frames can help students become writers of expository text. A writing frame is a template that includes key words and phrases specific for a particular text structure. The frame provides students with a scaffold for their writing. Then, as students become more familiar with a text structure, the writers internalize the writing frame and it is no longer needed. Figure 5.3B shows a discussion writing frame.

Application and Example

In Mary Ann's sixth-grade class, students were having difficulties with their new social studies textbook. They seldom read their assignments and consistently did poorly on exams. However, they were able to read novels at their grade level.

Mary Ann did a readability check on the text and found that it ranged from fifth to eighth grade. Upon closer examination, she noticed that the

---

A Discussion Frame

There is a lot of discussion about whether _____ .

The people who agree with this idea, such as _____ ,

claim that _____ .

They also argue that _____ .

A further point they make is _____ .

However there are also strong arguments against this point of view.

_____ believe that _____ .

Another counterargument is _____ .

Furthermore _____ .

After looking at the different points of view and the evidence for them

I think _____ ,

because _____ .

FIGURE 5.3B   Discussion Frame. (Discussion frame from Wray, David, & Lewis, Maureen (1998, May). An approach to factual writing. *Reading Online*. Newark, DE: International Reading Association. Reprinted with permission).

authors often used the cause/effect and problem/solution text pattern in their writing. She decided to give her class a series of mini-lessons on these text patterns and the key or signal words found in the text.

One lesson involved the students in writing paragraphs about topics of their interest. In the paragraph they had to use signal words that helped the reader understand the word *because.* Scott wrote the following:

> Lake Mead can be a fun place to play since it isn't polluted. Because almost no chemicals come into the lake, there is a plentiful supply of fish and very little algae. There are strict laws and high fines for dumping. As a result, people can enjoy the lake for recreation.

Teaching Aids and References for Understanding Text Structure

Reading Trail

http://www.everestquest.com/reading.htm

Strengthening Reading and Writing Skills Using the Internet

http://teacher.scholastic.com/professional/teachtech/internetreadwrite.htm

Literacy Matters

http://www.literacymatters.org/content/text/intro.htm

Text Structure

http://www.nea.org/reading/usingtextstructure.html

Just Read Now

http://www.justreadnow.com/index.htm

Pearson, P. D., & Camperell, K. (1994). Comprehension of text structures. In R. B. Ruddell, M. R. Ruddell, & H. Singer (Eds.), *Theoretical models and process of reading.* Delaware: International Reading Association.

Petersen, M. (1998). The virtual learning environment: The design of a website for language learning. *Computer Assisted Language Learning, 11,* 363–379.

Pinnell, G. S., & Jaggar, A. M. (1991). Oral language: Speaking and listening in the classroom. In J. Flood, J. Jensen, D. Lapp, & R. J. Squire (Eds.), *Handbook of research on teaching the English language arts.* Urbana, IL: National Council of Teachers of English; Newark, DE: International Reading Association.

Ryder, R. J., & Graves, M. F. (1998). *Reading and learning in content areas.* Upper Saddle River, NJ: Prentice Hall.

Smith, F. (1983). *Essays into literacy: Selected papers and some afterthoughts.* Portsmouth, NH: Heinemann.

Taylor, B. M. (1992). Text structure, comprehension, and recall. In S. J. Samuels & A. E. Fartstrup (Eds.), *What research has to say about reading instruction* (2nd ed.). Newark, DE: International Reading Association.

Tonjes, M. J. Wolpow, R., & Zintz, M. V. (1999). *Integrated content literacy.*
New York: The McGraw-Hill Publishers.

Wray, D., & Lewis, M. (May, 1998). An approach to factual writing.
Reading On Line Available:

http://www.readingonline.org/articles

CONCEPT-ORIENTED READING INSTRUCTION

Concept-oriented reading instruction (CORI) is organized around a broad conceptual theme that integrates science and language arts (Guthrie & McCann, 1977). CORI consists of the following instructional characteristics: conceptual theme, observation, self-direction, strategies, collaboration, self-expression, and coherence. This strategy helps struggling readers to better understand the text they read as well as increase student motivation to engage in literacy activities.

The Power of Concept-Oriented Reading Instruction for Struggling Readers

- The social component allows for students to engage in a cooperative learning process where their thoughts and the thoughts of their peers can intermingle to clarify points and improve comprehension.

- By capitalizing on students' interest in a topic, you can help them make mental connections to prior knowledge and stimulate their curiosity and openness to new ideas.

- Struggling readers are provided with concrete examples that can be used to build more abstract thinking and understand complex text.

Steps to Follow

1. *Conceptual theme.*   Select a broad conceptual theme from the science curriculum; for example, life cycles.

2. *Observation.*   Provide a real-life experience with concrete objects, while teaching and modeling strategies for observation. This step leads to student questioning and motivation. Allow time for discussions and journal reflections.

3. *Self-direction.*   Provide a framework with choices of topics, tasks, and media for learning. Provide scaffolding, resources, and goals for activities. Students take responsibility for their own learning by making choices.

4. *Strategies.*   Serve as a coach, engaging students through modeling, peer tutoring, and whole-class discussions on the selection and use of strategies. The emphasized strategies are problem finding, using prior knowledge, searching for information, comprehending informational text, self-monitoring, and interpreting literacy text.

5. *Collaboration.*   Provide for social structures that include not only individual work but also small groups of teams, partnerships, and

whole group activities. Provide support for collaborative work by assisting and monitoring students listening to others, respecting perspectives, and using information from each other.

6. *Self-expression.* Allow students to select the topic or style of communication. Students may choose to create posters, make videos, write, or perform.

7. *Coherence.* Coherence is inherent to the CORI instructional framework, as students participate in the activities that link real-life experiences to conceptual understanding.

Using Concept-Oriented Reading Instruction with English Language Learners

As you gather materials for the study of a broad conceptual theme, you will construct a text set of content and literature books about the topic. Freeman and Freeman (2000) discussed the importance of using text sets with English language learners:

(a) Books of different difficulty levels provide an avenue for students to participate fully in discussions;

(b) Naturally repeated vocabulary in thematic book sets allows for development of both English and reading proficiency;

(c) In-depth concepts and broadened perspectives are developed as books related to a common theme are read; and

(d) A variety of response activities leads to critical thinking and a deeper understanding of the topic.

Peregoy and Boyle (2000) offered six criteria for organizing thematic instruction for the promotion of language development, critical thinking, independence, and interpersonal collaboration for English language learners. The six recommended criteria are all apparent in CORI: (a) meaning and purpose, (b) building on prior experience, (c) integrated opportunities to use oral and written language for learning purposes, (d) scaffolding for support, (e) collaboration, and (f) variety.

Improving Writing Through Concept-Oriented Reading Instruction

The reading-writing connection is strongly enhanced by the CORI strategy. As students are immersed in a content topic, the vocabulary, concepts, and facts learned through reading and discussions will naturally flow into their writing. You should become knowledgeable about developing text sets to support students' inquiries. School library databases can be scoured for books to include in text sets. To encourage trying different writing forms, students can keep a checklist of genres in their writing folders. In addition to the different genres of fiction, they should experiment with a variety of expository text structures as well.

As students check off the different genres and structures on their lists, they will see their own growing repertoire of authorship.

Application and Examples

Using life cycles as a broad conceptual theme, introduce plants with a real-life experience with seeds. Provide a variety of fruits and vegetables for the students to investigate. They can begin by predicting and estimating the size and number of seeds. As the items are cut up and seeds are examined, many questions will be raised. Provide the students with a wide variety of students' literature that lends itself to the investigation of seeds and plants. Include all genres; some students may want to read contemporary realistic fiction, folk tales, legends, or science fiction about plants as they become immersed in the topic. Assist students in acquiring access to other media to investigate plant life.

Teaching Aids and References for Concept-Oriented Reading Instruction

Freeman, D. E., & Freeman, Y. S. (2000). *Teaching reading in multilingual classrooms.* Portsmouth, NH: Heinemann.

Guthrie, J. T., & McCann, A. D. (1997). Characteristics of classrooms that promote motivations and strategies for learning. In J. T. Guthrie & A. Wigfield (Eds.), *Reading engagement: Motivating readers through integrated instruction.* Newark, DE: International Reading Association.

Peregoy, S. F., & Boyle, O. W. (2000). *Reading, writing, & learning in ESL: A resource book for K–12 teachers.* New York: Longman.

READING PICTURES

The old adage, " a picture is worth a thousand words," comes to mind when considering ways to assist struggling readers to comprehend text. Readers' comprehension of a text is enhanced through the use of picture clues. These picture clues may be in the form of photographs, illustrations, charts, tables, or other graphics. It is important that students learn to "read" pictures and other forms of graphic representations since comprehension is enhanced when these images are included in text (Glazer, 1998).

Young students are encouraged to use picture clues to gain meaning from narrative text. Good picture books are those in which the illustrations and text work in tandem: Many readers may find expository text more challenging than narrative because of the author's writing style and complex concepts and ideas, as well as the readers' overall inexperience with expository text structure. While today's textbooks and nonfiction books include many forms of pictorial representations to assist readers, these texts still prove challenging and require you to instruct students in how to "read the pictures."

The growing use of technology in our society has caused educators to broaden our definition of literacy to include viewing. As defined in the *Standards for English Language Arts* (1996), viewing is attending to communication conveyed by visual representations. The media for these communications include television, video and film, and hypermedia. Related to the viewing is the development of visual literacy.

Visual literacy is an emerging area of study that deals with what we see and how we interpret it. This is approached from a range of disciplines that: (a) study the physical processes involved in visual perception; (b) use technology to represent visual imagery; and (c) develop intellectual strategies used to interpret and understand what is seen (Pennings, 2003). Focus your teaching efforts on helping students develop strategies for reading pictures and the relationship between pictures and text.

The Power of Reading Pictures for Struggling Readers

▪ Readers learn how pictures help clarify text information.

▪ Readers learn to integrate text and pictures to obtain meaning.

▪ Readers learn that authors may rely on pictures to give their text fuller meaning.

▪ Readers who have been unsuccessful with traditional text may be motivated to learn because other media are involved.

Steps to Follow

1. Begin with something that is familiar to students, such as a picture from a newspaper or magazine that has a caption. Select a picture that shows people interacting or reacting rather than a snapshot of an individual. Photographs from current newspapers and magazines as well as historical photographs found in textbooks, photo essay publications, and Internet websites are excellent sources for this strategy.

2. Show the picture to a group of students with the caption masked. Ask the students to look at the picture carefully for a few minutes and try to mentally compose an explanation for what is happening in the picture. Instruct them to look at all areas of the picture for details and helpful information.

3. Depending on the age of the students, have them individually or collectively write as much as possible to explain what is happening in the picture.

4. Have the students then read the caption and compare it with their ideas. Since captions are intended to be short explanations for pictures or illustrations, the students will usually generate much more text. This reinforces the importance of pictures as they read and view.

5. Once the students are comfortable with photographs, follow a similar plan for "reading" illustrations, posters, and graphs. The more abstract the representation, the more direct teaching is needed.

Using Reading Pictures with English Language Learners

You may want to adopt a set of questions to stimulate discussion with ELL students. These questions can be posted in the classroom and used as a reference for small group discussion:

What is the main subject of this picture?

What is going on in this picture?

What do you see that makes you say that?

When do you think this picture was taken?

What happened right before the photograph was taken?

What do you think happened just after the photograph was taken?

Would you have liked to be in this picture? Why or why not?

Improving Writing with Reading Pictures

For students who often are at a loss for what to write, the availability of a picture library in the classroom can be helpful to stimulate ideas. Begin your picture libraries by collecting current event photos from the local newspaper. Individual photos can be placed inside the lower half of a file folder and then run through a laminator. Students can contribute to the classroom picture library by bringing pictures from magazines or even family photos (with parental permission, of course).

Historical pictures from Internet sites as well as history and social studies textbooks can also be used to stimulate ideas for writing. Students can find an interesting picture and then use the previous discussion questions to guide their writing.

Finally, while it is very common for young students to draw pictures as part of their writing, older students, who struggle with writing, should be encouraged to "draw" as part of the prewriting or brainstorming stage of the writing process. You can model how the use of stick figures and simple shapes may help an idea evolve into something worth writing about. The point here is not to use drawing to accompany a piece of writing but to use drawing to stimulate the production of text.

Application and Example

Laura, one of the interns at the Paradise Professional Development School, was assigned to work with a group of five fourth graders who were reading at the third-grade instructional level. The classroom teacher told Laura that these students were having a great deal of difficulty working on their social studies projects on the states because they couldn't read most of the nonfiction or reference books in the classroom.

Before meeting with the students, Laura looked through the materials in the classroom. While it was true that the text was difficult, most of the books were filled with photographs, graphs, charts, and illustrations that the students could use to complete their projects. Laura decided to show the students how to "read the pictures."

The next day when Laura met with the five students, she showed them a picture from the newspaper with the caption removed. She told them:

> You can learn a great deal from pictures if you study them closely. Authors use pictures to help better explain what they have written or to show the information in a different way. Take a look at this picture from the newspaper. Study it carefully for a few minutes and try to figure out what is going on. Pretend you are a detective looking for clues. When you have some ideas, write them down so we can share them.

The picture Laura provided showed approximately 100 adults in a toy store pushing and shoving as they try to buy a popular Christmas toy. The store manager and clerks are trying hard to hand the toys to as many people as possible without being "mobbed."

After the students had several minutes to work independently, Laura asked them to each tell their ideas about the picture. Using a language experience approach form (see Part III), Laura wrote down the students' ideas on a piece of chart paper (see Figure 5.4).

Laura then told the students to think about what they all said about the picture and then to read the caption she had written on another sheet of chart paper.

"Let's compare what the caption says with what we said about the picture," Laura instructed the students. "What is the same? What is different?"

The students commented that they were right about the people wanting a special toy and that the shoppers were pushing to get them. Laura then pointed out that the caption is a summary of what is happening in the picture but that the students had told much more about the picture. "There is an old saying that says one picture is worth a thousand words," Laura told them. "Look at how much you understood by looking at the picture carefully."

Teaching Aids and References for Reading Pictures

Picture This. (2003). Oakland Museum of California
http://www.museumca.org/picturethis/index.html

Tara said, "I think all these people are trying to buy something that is very cheap."

David said, "This looks like a supermarket or toy store and everyone wants to buy the same thing right away."

Alana said, "There is one lady who looks very worried, like she might not be able to get the toy."

Enrico said, "The people behind the counter look very tired, especially the man in the baseball cap."

Wesley said, "I think some people are pushing and some may get hurt."

FIGURE 5.4   Reading as Picture Ideas.

Reading Pictures: Guardian Resources
http://www.learn.co.uk

Freefotos
http://www.freefoto.com/

Visual Literacy
http://www.academic.marist.edu/pennings/vislit2.htm

Visual Literacy and Picture Books
http://falcon.jmu.edu/~ramseyil/picture.htm

Glazer, S. M. (1998). *Assessment in instruction: Reading, writing, spelling and phonics for all learners.* Norwood, MA: Christopher-Gordon.

Hibbing, A. E., & Rankin-Erickson, J. L. (2003). A picture is worth a thousand words: Using visual images to improve comprehension for middle school struggling readers. *The Reading Teacher, 56,* 758–770.

National Council of Teachers of English and International Reading Association Standards for English Language Arts, (1996), Newark: DE NCTE and IRA.

Pennings, A. (2003) Visual Literacy. Retrieved 11/26/04

http://www.academic.marist.edu/pennings/vislit2.htm

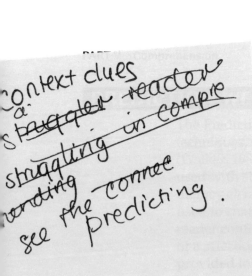

on Web is a combination of two modified instructional
iterature webbing (Norton, 1985) and prediction maps
). Literature webbing was presented as a structure to be
dents' trade books; it is a visual representation of the
nts of a story (Reutzel & Fawson, 1989). Prediction maps are
the comprehension process of prediction and revision, as the
ns, revises, or expands predictions throughout the reading
Walker, 1996). A template for the Prediction Web is
e Appendix, Form 6.

of Prediction Webs and Charts for Struggling Readers

- The strategy allows the struggling reader to predict words, phrases, or events that will occur in the selection. This is done before the reading begins and continues throughout the reading session.
- The reader combines the knowledge of story structure with picture and semantic clues to predict vocabulary usage and story events. The power of the strategy lies in its allowance for revision and extension of predictions as the reader progresses through the text.

Steps to Follow

1. Using a selection that is at the readers' instructional level, preview it with the students. Use the title, cover, and illustrations to prompt discussion.

2. Begin the web by writing the title in a cloud shape in the middle of a plain sheet of paper.

3. Ask the students for general ideas or ask specific questions that lend themselves to predictions. Example: What do you think will happen first in the story? What do you think is happening on this page? Do you know what that item is called?

4. Write the readers' predictions in web style around the perimeter of the cloud title.

5. Ask the students to read to a designated page in the selection.

6. Together discuss the story to that point. Direct the students' attention to the predictions noted on the web. The students then confirm which predictions were correct. Together discuss why it seemed likely that a certain prediction might have come true, and what was different in the story that led to a different outcome.

7. Next, ask the students to revise or expand predictions for the next segment of the story.

8. Continue this process throughout the reading, as you and the students discuss literacy elements (characters, setting, plot, and

themes), along with story structure (beginning, middle, and end) and vocabulary words.

Using Prediction Webs and Charts with English Language Learners

Combining prereading predictions with a graphic web or chart integrates two effective practices to enhance comprehension for ELL students. Farnan, Flood, and Lapp (1994) explained webbing as a structure that students can utilize not only to access and organize ideas, but also to actively connect what is known to what is new. This is especially important for ELL students, as vocabulary is highlighted along with connections between predictions and concepts. Peregoy and Boyle (2001) underscored the importance of developing vocabulary before students read a text and using pictures or diagrams whenever possible.

Dottie used a prediction web with a group of English language learners preparing to read a preprimer book, *Secret Soup.* First, on a piece of 12 × 18 white construction paper, Dottie wrote "Secret Soup" in a cloud shape in the middle of the paper. Her students told her the Spanish word for soup, *sopa,* which was then also written in the cloud. Around the web, Dottie wrote whatever her students predicted about the book (see Figure 5.5A).

After the predictions were recorded, the group read the book together. As they read, they returned to the web from time to time to confirm or revise their predictions. If they confirmed that a word they had predicted was in the story, it was starred. Following the reading, the students used the Prediction Web to write their own story about secret soup. They could use any or all of the words that had been recorded on the Prediction Web.

Improving Writing with Prediction Webs and Charts

Prediction Webs and charts facilitate a smooth connection from reading to writing. The ELL students who read about "secret soup" were able to

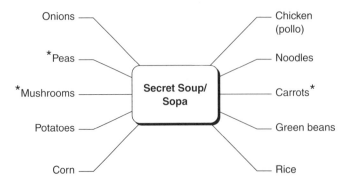

FIGURE 5.5A   Prediction Web for "Secret Soup/Sopa."

utilize the prediction map for their reading experience as a catalyst to their writing experience. The web provided the ideas and concepts about the secret soup story, and it also provided vocabulary that could be used in a new story about soup. A similar process of clustering was described by Peregoy and Boyle (2001) as a strategy that allows writers to develop vocabulary and prepare to write. The following features of cluster use are pointed out as advantages: (a) They are created freely by the student with no rules or parameters; (b) They are easy to share, allowing the student to create the story orally; and (c) They are an effective tool that evolves with students' literacy development.

Application and Examples

The Prediction Web can be used with books at any level. Another group of Dottie's students, reading at a beginning second-grade level, used a prediction strategy chart with another book about soup. The selection was *Spectacular Stone Soup.* Using the book cover and their prior knowledge of soup, the students made predictions for the beginning, middle, and end of the story. (See Figure 5.5B.) Next, the students skimmed through the book, looking at the handful of illustrations. Then they made a second set of predictions, which Dottie wrote under the previous predictions. As the group read each chapter, they revisited the prediction chart, confirming, revising, or expanding both sets of predictions.

	Spectacular Stone Soup		
	Beginning	**Middle**	**End**
First Predictions	It might have carrots and beans in it.	It's not really stone soup.	It makes the kids toothless when they start eating it.
	It might have rocks in it.	It won't taste good.	The kids are happy because the soup smells good.
Second Predictions	There's a map.	A boy is looking for something in the cupboard.	There's a stove that plugs into the wall with a pot of soup on it.
	There are onions in the soup.	A girl is yelling at the kids.	The teacher is cooking soup.
	The kids are drawing.	A boy yells at the girl for drinking the water.	

FIGURE 5.5B Prediction Chart for "Spectacular Stone Soup."

Teaching Aids and References for Prediction Webs and Charts

Farnan, N., Flood, J., & Lapp, D. (1994). Comprehending through reading and writing: Six research-based instructional strategies. In K. Spangenberg-Urbschat & R. Pritchard (Eds.), *Kids come in all languages: Reading instruction for ESL students.* Newark, DE: International Reading Association.

Norton, D. (1985). *The effective teaching of language arts.* Columbus, OH: Merrill.

Peregoy, S. F., & Boyle, O. F. (2001). *Reading, writing, & learning in ESL: A resource book for K–12 teachers.* New York: Longman.

Reutzel, D. R., & Fawson, P. C. (1989). Using a literature webbing strategy lesson with predictable books. *The Reading Teacher, 43,* 208–215.

Walker, B. J. (1985). Right-brained strategies for teaching comprehension. *Academic Therapy, 21,* 133–141.

Walker, B. J. (1996). *Diagnostic teaching of reading: Techniques for instruction and assessment.* Englewood Cliffs, NJ: Merrill.

Children's Book References

Giff, P. R. (1989). *Spectacular stone soup.* New York: Dell.

Hessell, J. (1989). *Secret soup.* Auckland, NZ: Rigby.

WHERE'S THE QUESTION?

"Do you take the bus or carry your lunch to school?"

That's a question Maria's uncle asked her as a child to make her laugh. When she first heard the question, she tried to answer it with a "yes" or "no," but soon found out that those responses didn't work. Later, she realized the language absurdity of the question and laughed.

As teachers, we are well aware of the importance of asking "good questions" as well as the fact that we have asked our students to answer questions that to them may have appeared to be as absurd as Maria's uncle's question. But what makes a good question? A simple but significant answer is that a good question causes students to think. Christenbury and Kelly (1983) suggested that questioning as an instructional technique can:

1. Provide students with an opportunity to find out what they think by hearing what they say.

2. Allow students to explore topics and argue points of view.

3. Give students the opportunity to interact among themselves.

4. Give teachers immediate information about student comprehension and learning.

Over the years, researchers have shown that questioning aids students in the comprehension of text as well as composition of their own text because questioning helps students sharpen their critical thinking skills. You can capitalize on this highly used teaching technique by taking the time to formulate questions that push students' thinking beyond the obvious. This is especially true for struggling readers.

Some teachers tend to ask struggling readers only "low level" questions because the students have difficulty with "reading the text." These questions prevent struggling readers from ever getting into the heart of a good story and give them the impression that reading is memorizing as many details as possible. While details are important, teachers can overshadow the author's message if details are given too much attention. Understanding why the old woman in the story wore a black dress and discussing the possible reasons will enhance students' overall comprehension of a story more than just recalling that the woman's dress was black.

A number of questioning strategies have been developed that were intended to improve reading comprehension. For example, Manzo (1969, 1985) developed the ReQuest Procedure in which a teacher models questions based on a short segment of text for a group of students who then ask questions of the teacher. Raphael's QARs (1982) and ReQARs (1986) help students understand the relationship between questions and answers within a given text. Answers to questions are classified as "in the book" or "in my head." The teacher models the strategy and gradually turns over more responsibility to the students to ask and answer questions.

At the Literacy Development Center, tutors are encouraged to engage students in conversation and discussion that naturally include questioning. This is not an easy thing to do because many of our students have learned the "game" of answering questions: only make eye contact when you know the answer. For some struggling readers the question/answer recitation process that some teachers use is an anxiety-provoking situation. We try to avoid this by using a more instructional and conversational approach, which we call "Where's the Question?" This strategy was named by one of the students at the Center who kept waiting for the tutor to ask something and finally said rather exasperatedly, "So where's the question?"

The Power of "Where's The Question?" for Struggling Readers

- This strategy allows students to hear an adult model book conversation over time. The students are then invited to talk about the book or story and become the teacher, as is done in the previously mentioned strategies.

- The students' anxiety level is lowered because they see the activity as talking and game-like rather than answering questions about what they just read.

- In addition, students are free to choose a text of interest within the independent reading level when first learning the strategy. This strategy works best with students who have an established rapport with a teacher or tutor.

Steps to Follow

1. Have a student select a book of interest that can be read independently. Based on your knowledge of a child's interests, the selection may be made from a small group of preselected books.

2. Instruct the child to read it silently in its entirely or, depending on its length, the first chapter, while you follow along or read from a separate copy. Encourage the child to ask for assistance with any unknown words.

3. Begin the conversation with some overall comment about the book but do not ask the child anything; instead, wait between comments to give the child the chance to "add to the conversation. "

4. It is possible that some students will not respond the first time. That's okay. Have other books ready or go on and read the next chapter. Tell the child that he or she will be talking about the book the next time.

5. If the child is not ready to talk about the book after a reasonable period of wait time, model again for the child and invite the child by saying, "Your turn."

6. If the child still is unable to talk about the book without specific guidance, begin with a request that will elicit a personal response to the text, such as, "Tell me about the part you like the best. "

7. This strategy takes time for students to learn; be patient and return to it at a later date if it is not immediately successful.

8. Ultimately, small groups of students will carry on their own discussion without much involvement from you.

Using "Where's the Question? " with English Language Learners

The purpose of this strategy is to encourage students to discuss a book that they have enjoyed. In this sense, it is similar to what adults do when talking to one another about a new best seller. The focus is on oral language and how to engage in a discussion. English language learners will benefit from listening to a teacher and student or two students engaged in discussion. One adaptation that can be easily employed is to tape record a "Where's the Question" session through which a good model is presented. Then, the second language learner can listen for the language structures that are used in the discussion such as: "My favorite character was _____ because _____ ." or "I really like the part when _____ ."

Improving Writing with "Where's the Question?"

As shown in the Application and Example section, "Where's the Question?" provides another vehicle for students to connect oral language with written language. Struggling writers can also make use of the tape recorder to hear their conversation and use it as the basis for their writing. Teachers would need to provide instructional support as students transform dialogue/discussion to an expository text structure.

Application and Example

Tracy had been tutoring Rosa for four weeks. Rosa, a fifth grader who was having difficulty with understanding text at grade level, enjoyed folk tales. Tracy brought copies of several different folk tales to the next tutoring session. Rosa chose *The Mountain that Loved a Bird* by Alice McLerran, a picture book with text at approximately the fourth-grade level. Tracy explained to Rosa that this was the story of how a bird and its daughters visited a mountain year after year and helped the mountain to change. Then they read the book silently. "When we finish reading, we'll talk about the book, " Tracy told Rosa.

Tracy:	I really enjoyed that story. It was so interesting to see how the mountain first was just bare stone and then became so green and beautiful. (Tracy waited for about a minute before Rosa spoke.)
Rosa:	I liked the part when the mountain kept asking "Isn't there some way you could stay?" and Joy, the bird, said she would come back next year.
Tracy:	Yes, that was interesting. You know at first, I thought it was the same bird coming back but then I remembered the part that explained that birds don't live as long as mountains.
Rosa:	Yeah, and then the mountain started to cry after the 100th time and the tears turned into waterfalls.
Tracy:	It is very interesting how the author used a folk tale to explain how rock becomes soil.
Rosa:	I didn't get that part.

At this point Tracy turned to the text and showed Rosa the passage and assisted her in comprehending that part of the story by "breaking down the text. "

Tracy:	Is there any other part of the story you wanted to talk more about?
Rosa:	Well, I did like the illustrations.

Tracy followed Rosa's lead and took time to go back into the book to examine Eric Carle's illustrations and discuss how they helped relate the story. Tracy suggested that Rosa write a short summary of the story and try to illustrate it like Eric Carle. Rosa's work appears in Figure 5.6.

The Mountain That Loved A Bird
by Alice McLerran

This is a great story! Long ago a bird flew to a bare mountain. The mountain was lonely and wanted the bird to stay. The bird's name was Joy. She couldn't stay but said she would send her daughters to visit the mountain. When the birds came, they brought seeds. Slowly the bare mountain became green and beautiful. Finally there were tall trees and the bird stayed. She could build her nest!

FIGURE 5.6   Story Summary from "Where's the Question?" Strategy.

Teaching Aids and References For "Where's The Question?"

Almasi, J. F., McKeown, M. G., & Beck, I. L. (1996). The nature of engaged reading in classroom discussion of literature. *Journal of Literacy Behavior, 28*, 107–146.

Christenbury, L., & Kelly, P. (1983). *Questioning: A path to critical thinking.* Urbana, IL: Eric Clearinghouse on Reading and Communication and National Council of Teachers of English.

Goldenberg, C. (1992/1993). Instructional conversations: Promoting comprehension through discussion. *The Reading Teacher, 46,* 316–326.

Manzo, A. (1969). The ReQuest procedure. *Journal of Reading, 13,* 123–127.

Manzo, A. V. (1985). Expansion models for the ReQuest, CAT, GRP and REAP reading/study procedures. *Journal of Reading, 28,* 498–502.

Morgan, N., & Saxton, J. (1994). *Asking better questions: Models, techniques and classroom activities for engaging students in learning.* Membrok, Ontario: Pembroke Publishers.

Raphael, T. E. (1982). Teaching children question-answering strategies. *The Reading Teacher, 36,* 186–191.

Raphael, T. E. (1986). Teaching question-answering relationships revisited. *The Reading Teacher, 39,* 516–523.

Children's Book References

McLerran, A. (1985). *The mountain that loved a bird.* New York: Scholastic, Inc.

Teachers on Teaching:

http://www.ncrel.org/he/tot

WORKING WITH MIDDLE SCHOOL STUDENTS TO IMPROVE COMPREHENSION: CONCEPT MAPS

Students in middle schools or junior high school settings are often required to read textbooks independently. Their ability to comprehend new concepts and ideas is paramount to students' success during these adolescent years. The previously suggested strategies in this chapter may be adapted for almost any grade level and text for either developmental reading or remedial reading purposes.

Alvermann (2001) urges subject area teachers to provide literacy instruction that is developmentally, culturally, and linguistically responsive to their needs. This is most effective when reading and writing instruction is part of the subject matter instruction. So, for example, good science teachers include instruction in how to read and write like a scientist when middle students are engaged in science inquiry.

Middle school students will find concept maps a useful tool for comprehending complex text. Concept maps are diagrams that graphically illustrate the relationships among key ideas in text. Perkins (1992) suggests that pictorial languages of thinking, such as concept maps, are advantageous in that they enable students to simplify complex patterns of ideas.

Power of the Strategy

- Comprehension of text is enhanced through a pictorial representation of key ideas and the relationships between ideas.

- Concept maps may be used for instruction before, during, and/or after reading a text.

▪ Comprehension for English language learners is supported because concept maps provide a visual explanation of complex ideas as well as show how these ideas are organized (Peregoy & Boyle, 2001).

Steps to Follow

The following suggested steps are based on Novak's article (2001):

1. Select an area of knowledge that is common to your students. It could be something from the curriculum they have studied, plants, or something from the community such as "going to the supermarket. " Another way to approach concept maps is through questions and problem solving: What happens when bears hibernate?

2. Once the area of knowledge is identified, key vocabulary or concepts are listed. Post-It notes work well because the individual words or concepts can be moved when creating the map.

3. Concept maps show relationships between key vocabulary and concepts from the most general to the most specific. The vocabulary and concepts are arranged to show this relationship if possible. For example, Figure 5.7 is a concept map for water.

4. If available, computer software programs such as *Inspirations* allow the moving of concepts together with linking statements and also the moving of groups of concepts and links to restructure the map. These concept maps can be saved for later use, printed for others to see, and e-mailed to the teacher and/or other students.

5. Students can add to their concept maps when they learn new vocabulary or when a new link between ideas is found. It is important to reposition the concepts in ways that lead to clarity.

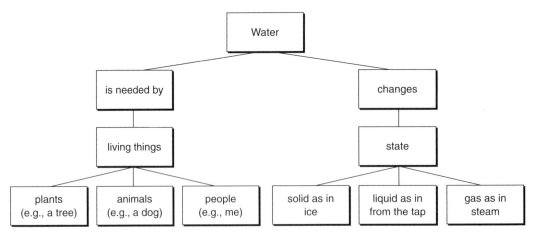

FIGURE 5.7   Example of a Concept Map.

Teaching Aids and Professional References

Houghton Mifflin English for Middle School Students
http://www.eduplace.com/kids/hme/6–8

Inspirations Software, Inc.

http://www.inspirations.com

Alvermann, D. E. (2001). *Effective literacy instruction for adolescents.* Executive Summary and Paper Commissioned by the National Reading Conference. Chicago, IL: National Reading Conference.

Novak, J. D. (2001). Cornell University Institute for Human and Machine Cognition: Concept Mapping the Theory Underlying Concept Maps and How to Construct Them. http://cmap.coginst.uwf.edu

Novak, J. D., & Gowin, D. B. (1984). *Learning how to learn.* New York and Cambridge, UK: Cambridge University Press.

Peregoy, S. F., & Boyle, O. F. (2001). *Reading, writing, and learning in ESL: A resource book for K–12 teachers.* New York: Addison Wesley Longman, Inc.

Perkins, D. (1992). *Smart schools.* New York: Free Press.

ASSESSING COMPREHENSION

How do you know when someone knows something? We most often ask questions of our students, but we also know that the quality of the question determines the quality of the answer. We also know that understanding can take place on many levels. For example, think about a third grader's understanding of the word *liberty* when singing "America (My Country 'Tis of Thee)" and the understanding of the word by a political prisoner. Both comprehend the words but their depth of understanding differs considerably.

One of the most powerful assessment tools we have used is "retelling." Previously, we discussed retelling as an instructional teaching strategy. As an assessment tool, retelling focuses on a child's ability to reconstruct the important elements of a story. Insight is gained into a child's ability to comprehend a given text, sense of story, and language complexity. Retelling as an assessment tool is most useful when assessing students' understanding of narrative text.

Morrow (1988) described the retelling of stories as a diagnostic tool in great detail. It has also been incorporated into informal reading inventories such as Flynt and Cooter's *Reading Inventory for the Classroom* (2001) as well as a topic included in most literacy methods textbooks. A child may retell a story after it is read to the child or after the child reads it independently. We suggest the following steps:

1. Select an appropriate book for the child. A book should have a good plot structure and easily discernible events. If the story is read independently by the child, make sure the story is at the child's independent reading level. More able and older students (grades 3 and above) may retell a chapter from a longer book.

2. Tell the student before reading or listening to the selection that he/she will be asked to retell it.

3. For purposes of assessment, it is best to tape record the student's retelling for later reference and analysis.

4. It is crucial to allow the student to retell the story without prompts. Some students may need some initial encouragement or an occasional "anything else?" The book should be closed before the student begins the retelling.

5. A student may retell a story orally or in writing.

Once students have completed the retelling, you can analyze the response in a variety of ways. Form 7 in the Appendix is a story retelling assessment form that is easy to use. It includes story components and oral presentations. Make sure to tell students before the retelling process begins if they will be evaluated on both areas, because oral presentation would involve some rehearsal by the students, or only the story components. Weighted scoring may also be used if a numeric result is needed.

Garcia (1994) recommends using retelling in conjunction with story maps to assess second language learners. ELL students should be allowed to use their first language until they have enough facility with English to convey their ideas. Story maps that include characters, setting, problem, events, and resolution provide a structure that you can assess in a manner similar to what was previously described.

As for assessing student comprehension of expository text, concept mapping, as previously described, can be easily adapted to determine understanding of science, social studies, and mathematical concepts. For example, you can ask students to begin a concept map that includes important vocabulary and links associated with a given topic such as "The Writing of the Declaration of Independence." Collect the maps and assess the students' prior knowledge of the topic; a simple point system can be used to note both "correct" links as well as misconceptions. Keep a record of the students' scores on a spreadsheet. Then, have the students read text that provides details about the Declaration of Independence. Using a different color pencil or pen, ask the students to add or modify their concept maps to reflect their new understandings of the topic. Evaluate the maps a second time and use the assessment results to plan for individual and group instruction.

Professional References

Flynt, E. S., & Cooter, R. B. (2001). *Reading Inventory for the Classroom.* Upper Saddle River, NJ: Prentice Hall.

Garcia, G. E (1994). Assessing the literacy development of second-language students: A focus on authentic assessment. In Spangenberg-Urbschat, K., & Pritchard, R. (Eds.), *Kids come in all languages: Reading instruction for ESL students.* Newark, DE: International Reading Association.

Morrow, L. (1988). Retelling stories as a diagnostic tool. In Glazer, S., Seafoss, L., & Gentile, L. (Eds.), *Reexamining reading diagnosis: New trends and procedures.* Newark, DE: International Reading Association.

Soderman, A., Gregory, K., & O'Neill, L. (1999). *Scaffolding emergent literacy: A child-centered approach to PreK–Grade 5.* Boston: Allyn & Bacon.

APPENDIX

Additional Forms

May Be Reproduced for Classroom Use

FORM 6

Prediction Web Template

FORM 7

Story Retelling Assessment

Student's Name _____ Grade _____

Observer _____ Setting _____

Date	Summary of Observed Behavior	Implications

FORM 1A   Observation Form.

Literacy Interview

Name _____ Date _____

Grade _____ Given by _____

(1) What is reading?

(2) Why do people read?

(3) What is writing?

(4) Why do people write?

(5) A long time ago people could not read or write. How do you think people came to invent reading and writing?

FORM 1B The Literacy Interview. *(Meyerson, 1997.) (May be copied for classroom use.)*

The Goldilocks Plan

Is your book too hard, too easy, or just right for you?

Use the Goldilocks Plan to find out! Ask yourself these questions.

FORM 2A The Goldilocks Plan. *(Ohlhausen, M. M., & Jepsen, M. (1992). Lessons from Goldilocks: "Somebody's been choosing my books but I can make my own choices now!"* The New Advocate, 5, 31–46. Continued.

Too Hard?

If you answer "yes," this book is probably "too hard" for you. Give this book another try in a few months.

1. Are there more than two words on a page that you don't know?

2. Are you confused about what is happening in the book?

3. When you try to read a part out loud, does it sound choppy?

4. Will you have to ask someone to help with the book many times?

FORM 2B Continued.

Just Right?

If you answer "yes," this book is probably "just right" for you.
Go ahead. Read and learn from it.

1. Is this a new book for you?

2. Do you understand some of the book?

3. Are there just one or two words on a page that you don't know?

4. When you read out loud are some parts smooth and some choppy?

5. If you need help, will it just be now and then? Who can help you?

Too Easy?

If you answer "yes," this book is probably "too easy" for you. Have fun with it!

1. Have you read this book many, many times before?

2. Do you understand the story very well and can you tell someone about it almost as if you were the author?

3. Do you know how to say almost every word and what every word means?

4. Can you read the book out loud very smoothly?

Interviewer: _____   Interviewee: _____

1. What is your job at our school?

2. Where were you born?

3. Where did you go to elementary school?

4. What was your favorite grade?

5. Who was your favorite teacher?

6. What did you like most about school?

7. Why did you want to work in a school?

8. What's the best part about being in our school?

9. What are your hobbies?

10. Do you have any children?

11. What does your family do for fun?

12. Is there anything about yourself that you would like to add?

FORM 3 Biography Interview Questionnaire.

Words Per Minute

	200–
	195–
	190–
	185–
	180–
	175–
	170–
	165–
	160–
	155–
	150–
	145–
Words	140–
Per	135–
Minute	130–
	125–
	120–
	115–
	110–
	105–
	100–
	95–
	90–
	85–
	80–
	75–
	70–

Trial 1	Trial 2	Trial 3	Trial 4	Trial 5	Trial 6	Trial 7	Trial 8	Trial 9	Trial 10	Trial 11	Trial 12

Date:

Student: _____

FORM 4 Repeated Reading Graph.

Name _____

Title of book _____

Author _____

First time listening: Date completed _____

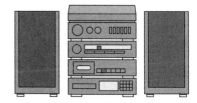

Listen to the story. Follow along with the reader. Enjoy the story.

Second time listening: Date completed _____

Listen to the story. Try to read the words with the reader.

Third time listening: Date completed _____

Listen to the story again and try to become the reader. Then read the book or a favorite part to someone.

FORM 5 Listening Center Activities.

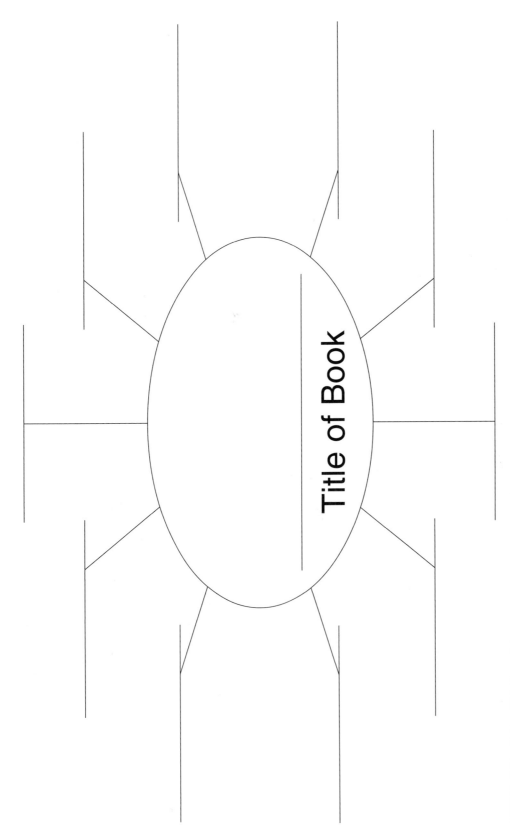

Title of Book

FORM 6 Prediction Web Template.

STORY RETELLING ASSESSMENT

Student's Name _____   Date _____

Retelling of _____

Story Component	Yes	No	Comments
Introduction (includes a beginning such as once upon a time, this is a story about, etc.)			
Main Characters (uses names of important characters in retelling)			
Setting (indicates place where and/or time when story occurred)			
Sequence of Events (tells story in order of events; is aware that sequence is important to retelling)			
Important Details (includes important details so that the story flows)			
Statement of Problem (indicates that there is some problem or conflict the main character(s) must solve or overcome)			
Resolution (includes statement regarding how problem or conflict is resolved and/or what happens to the main characters)			

Oral Presentation	Yes	No	Comments
Sentence Structure (uses complete sentences; avoids excessive use of "and then," "um," etc.)			
Vocabulary (uses story language; may include words or phrases directly from the story)			
Sense of Audience (is aware of telling the story to another person; may include listener with phrase such as "and do you know what happened next?")			
Use of Voice (uses a conversational tone; may also change voice to indicate characters)			

FORM 7 Story Retelling Assessment.

131